WESTMAR COLLEGE

P9-BAW-869

In Search of an Audience

In Search of an Audience

How an Audience Was Found
for the Tyrone Guthrie Theatre

Bradley G. Morison and Kay Fliehr

Commissioned by Associated Councils of the Arts

Preface by Sir Tyrone Guthrie

Pitman Publishing Corporation / New York · Toronto · London

PN
2277
,M55
T946

Copyright © 1968 by Associated Councils of the Arts
All rights reserved

Library of Congress Catalog Card Number: 68–18783
Manufactured in the United States of America
Designed by Martin Stephen Moskof & Assoc.

1.987654321

76210

Associated Councils of the Arts gratefully acknowledges the generous grant of Shell Companies Foundation which made possible the completion of this work.

4-13-70 B47 4.1(

Preface

Here is a modest and amusing account of how two people of
great goodwill and intelligence set about a new job. They were
to be the Publicity Department of a new kind of theatre. Very
rightly they realized that the sort of publicity which may serve
a Broadway production is unlikely to be efficient for a differ-
ently organized theatre with different aims.

They tried—perhaps the most difficult and strenuous activity in which we humans ever engage—to *think for themselves;* they tried to think in serious, sensible, and humane
terms what the theatre was trying to achieve, and why, and
how—and how they could contribute to its communal purpose.

As they rather ruefully mention, the theatre being a mul-
tifarious activity rarely reflects a single, pure, unfaltering
point of view. But how many human activities do? Political
organisms never, even under the most powerful and brilliant
of directors. I wonder whether the inspiration of the President
of General Motors is reflected in the action, still less the attitude, of each of the corporation's myriad employees. I doubt if
even the best organized military force completely expresses in
the heat of battle the best-laid plans of the most superb general. Somewhere along the line, confusions and misunderstand-
ings are bound to arise; and the success or failure of a campaign will hinge upon the ability of some young lieutenant to
think for himself in a tight corner. This makes me wonder

whether the chief task of leadership, be it in a military or civil context, is to create a "morale" which encourages all members of an organization to think for themselves to the limit of their capacity.

Morison and Fliehr had to express a policy which was not always clear, nor always consistent. They often had to guess what the policy was to which they were supposed to relate the public. This, you will rightly say, implies a failure in direction. But with a new enterprise, as this then was, it would not have been wise to have a hard-and-fast, doctrinaire policy. We had to grope our way towards not only what we *did*, but what we were trying to *be*. We were fully and clearly agreed upon the theatre's artistic policy and that the reason for the enterprise was to serve the public. But exactly how to relate ourselves to the public most usefully and efficiently we could not be clear; and I think, seeing how few precedents there were to guide us, that for the first few seasons we were right to play many of our tunes by ear.

What Morison and Fliehr have to say about the philosophy of their job seems to me extremely sensible and to reflect a deeper humanity and wider horizon than are usually associated with those whose task is to publicize and sell.

About some of the practical applications of this philosophy I am a little skeptical. It seems to me that with a limited staff and a limited budget there was rather too much reliance upon costly and time-consuming projects like Customer Research to cough up information which any reasonably experienced and sensible person already possesses; and much of which is anyway pretty irrelevant. Who cares if 14.7 percent of the audience in 1963 consisted of unmarried ladies between the ages of 18 and 35, whereas in 1966 the percentage was 14.4? Potentially this is significant as a guide to where publicity pressure must be applied. To vast firms with vast sales, and thence vast budgets for advertisement and image-making, this kind of research is important and valuable. Eventually the kind of information which these researches were designed to elicit will be valuable, even indispensable, to such organizations as ours. But the cost of the research ought, in my opinion, to be borne communally by many groups to whom it is relevant. While we

were, as we were in 1963, a lone pioneer in our field, I consider that this was spending beyond our means, and thinking
above our station. We should have relied less upon pseudo-
scientific researches ("pseudo" because the information can at
best only be approximate and is often at least as misleading as
no information), and more upon the good sense and good feeling of which this book is the warm-hearted evidence.

Sir Tyrone Guthrie

Foreword

What follows in this book is the history of a concentrated attack on what I believe to be the major problem facing the performing arts in this country today: the development of audiences. The attack took place at the Minnesota Theatre Company in Minneapolis, Minnesota: a new theatre which had its first performance in May of 1963. The Minnesota Theatre Company which performed in the Tyrone Guthrie Theatre, was conceived by three most disparate individuals: Tyrone Guthrie, Peter Zeisler, and myself. Contrary to the mood of the time when the theatre was conceived (1959), it was our deliberate conception to implant a full-grown "oak tree" of a theatre in Minnesota soil, the prevailing philosophy being that theatres should commence as "acorns" and gradually grow into "oak trees." The ensuing success of the Company is due in great part to the creative artistic endeavor of Tyrone Guthrie and others. But a theatre—like a symphony orchestra, ballet company, or art gallery—is an institution, and it is my strong belief that institutions survive in proportion to the efforts that they make toward community involvement.

This book does not concern itself with artistic questions, but I do not believe that there is one line in it that runs contrary to the artistic effort that was made in Minnesota. Quite the opposite; from my experience as managing director of the Minnesota Theatre Company from the time of its inception to

1966; from subsequent experience as member of the Rocke-feller Brothers Panel Report; and as president of the Theatre Communications Group, I fervently believe that the artistic continuity and even survival of any and all performing-arts in-stitutions depends upon the strength of each institution's ef-forts toward community involvement in the audience-develop-ment area.

The audience-development policies of the Minnesota The-atre Company for the first four years of its existence sprang from the highly creative minds of Mr. Morison and Mrs. Fliehr on whose experience this book is based. It does not purport to answer all questions. But I believe that the authors' actual ex-periences in Minneapolis are easily applicable to any and all other performing arts institutions.

Mr. Morison and Mrs. Fliehr brought a new insight to theatre, one which has long been missing and much needed. What is more, they never lost their sense of humor—a rarity in our somewhat pompous craft. Speaking quite personally, I believe my greatest reward from my many years with the Min-nesota Theatre Company came from working with Bradley Morison and Kay Fliehr.

Oliver Rea
New York, N.Y.

Contents

Prologue

THE ATTENDANCE RECORD of The Minnesota Theatre Company performing at the Tyrone Guthrie Theatre

Season	Season Tickets	Single Tickets	Total Attendance
1963 (20 weeks—4 plays)	21,295	98,751	183,931
1964 (24 weeks—4 plays)	19,483	136,698	214,630
1965 (28 weeks—5 plays)	16,614	173,377	239,833
1966 (28 weeks—5 plays)	15,928	134,452	214,172

This is not a "how-to-do-it" book. This is a "how-it-happened" story. It is the recounting of what occurred when a theatre burst full-blown upon a community on a grander scale than had ever before happened in this country, and when two professional public relations people were given the opportunity to explore new ways—and to make mistakes—on the same grand scale.

Ours was a unique opportunity, and from it came unique experiences. Because of the size of the Minnesota Theatre Company budget, manpower and money were available for more extensive activity in theatre audience-development than had previously been tried anywhere but on Broadway.

The public relations staff during most of the first four years consisted of two full-time professionals, a secretary, a part-time jack-of-all-trades, and, during several months of the year, a Ford Foundation administrative intern. The budget for public information and audience development ranged from about $85,000 in 1963—out of a total operating budget of $738,770—to approximately $140,000 in 1966 when overall expenditures were $1,012,286.

In the Midwest of 1963 there was an audience ready and waiting to buy tickets to Minnesota Theatre Company performances. This audience was sizeable enough so that we did not have to devote every bit of our daily energy to filling seats for the next night. This breathing room allowed us to look ahead and to make small beginnings toward developing larger, more broadly based audiences for the future.

Finally, and most importantly, our managing director, Oliver Rea, understood the need for a hard, new look at traditional theatrical-promotion practices. He provided an environment in which we were free to explore new concepts, and he encouraged us to do it.

With these opportunities open to us, we found ourselves with so many exciting possibilities that even an adequate staff and generous budget proved insufficient. Many projects which we knew should be carried out never were brought to fruition because of lack of time and money.

Nor was everything we tried successful. A look at the four-year, season- and single-ticket sales offers adequate proof that we did not discover a magic formula. Furthermore, there was not universal agreement among theatre people that our basic approaches were completely valid. The Minnesota Theatre Company itself decided at the end of the 1966 season to make a shift in emphasis in its promotion and audience-development efforts, and it was at that time that we decided our usefulness to the company had diminished.

In our search for new approaches to audience development, we did develop new opinions, new premises, and new questions about traditional methods. This book is an attempt to share these opinions, premises, and questions. While the Minnesota Theatre Company, and the circumstances under which it was created and is operating, are unique, we believe that many of the lessons learned from our experience can be of value to other theatres and, indeed, to other cultural institutions of all kinds. We hope that this recounting of those lessons may help to stimulate fresh and creative approaches to the relationship of artistic organizations to their audiences and their communities.

It should be noted here that very little comment is made in this book about artistic quality or the selection of plays for the repertory at the Tyrone Guthrie Theatre. The omission is not because we are unaware of the key influence which these factors have on attendance. It comes about because we do not believe that people charged with audience development should make judgments or comments on matters of artistic policy. Our job was only to educate an audience to appreciation of that policy.

Dominating the opinions which we developed during our four years' experience is the feeling that the arts, especially at this time in this country, require a totally new approach to what might loosely be called promotion. The traditions of theatrical press agentry, upon which most cultural institutions have often unwittingly based their public relations philosophy, seem dangerously outmoded.

It has long been considered a primary function of arts management to create an environment within an organization which is conducive to full growth and free expression of its creative talent. We believe that the primary function of public relations in today's arts organization must now be to create *an environment within the community* which is conducive to the full growth and free expression of the art and of the institution itself. A climate must be established which will encourage public acceptance of artistic policy, long- and short-range audience development, broad-based financial contribution, favorable governmental action, and the involved support of every part of the total community.

This concept of public relations encompasses far more than traditional press agentry. Meeting responsibilities of such scope will take new ideas and new people whose experience and points of view are as broad as the nature of the audience.

Now let us tell the story which led us to this opinion.

Bradley Morison
Kay Fliehr

Part One

In the Beginning . . .

I have suggested the reasons why we wanted the Twin Cities to support us. But reasons, I seem to have found out, are nearly always invented *after* a decision to defend, even excuse it. Inclinations, hunches have far more to do with crucial decisions than has reason.

. . . We *wanted* to work in the Twin Cities. Why? . . . We have discussed it often and we simply do not know.

SIR TYRONE GUTHRIE, *A New Theatre*

Chapter 1

Good Old Minn

The plane from Chicago poked its nose through a late afternoon overcast and eased onto the runway at Twin Cities International Airport. It was November 18, 1959. As the plane rolled to a stop, Tyrone Guthrie unfolded his six-foot-five-inch frame and escorted his wife down the ramp.

While greetings were exchanged with the welcoming committee, Dr. Guthrie's ever-searching eyes darted across the crowds and over the landscape, absorbing first impressions. In the car he turned in his seat ceaselessly—watching, listening, observing with the intensity of a man fascinated with life.

Walking into the hotel lobby, he leaned over to Oliver Rea who was accompanying him on their visit to the various cities which had expressed interest in a permanent repertory company.

"Oliver," he said, "I rather think I'm going to become quite fond of good old Minn."

The search for an audience for the theatre which would eventually be built in Minneapolis began the moment Sir Tyrone Guthrie set foot in "Good Old Minn." The events of that first day influenced the problems and opportunities with which the public relations department eventually had to wrestle.

The story of why Sir Tyrone, Oliver Rea, and Peter Zeisler set out in their search for a suitable place to establish a professional repertory theatre—and why, finally, they selected the Twin Cities of Minneapolis and St. Paul—has been told with eloquence and wit in Dr. Guthrie's book *A New Theatre*. It may be valuable to present some observations from the viewpoint of the authors of this book—two natives of the area who were not then involved, but who later became immersed in the frightening magnitude of what was begun on that November day in 1959.

There are those, including ourselves, who believe that Dr. Guthrie may have personally decided for the Twin Cities on that very day he first expressed fondness for "Good Old Minn." Not he, Rea, or Zeisler have ever claimed any completely rational reasons for the choice. Rea's decision was influenced in part, he thinks, by the personalities and vigor of the original steering committee that sought to capture the theatre for their city. Sir Tyrone does make some stabs at logic in his book, but he dismisses them as ways to justify an irrational decision. Many times we have heard him answer the question, "Why Minnesota?" with "Mostly hunch, dear fellow."

Now, hunch is the expression of instinct, and instinct lies at the heart of creative artistry. And if any hunch should be trusted without attempt at explanation, it should be that of this triumvirate. But it seems pertinent to this story to probe the reasons for this particular one.

The trio had set out upon their venture with the best of motives, yet harboring varying degrees of preconceived disdain for the unsophisticated "provinces" and their inhabitants. Much of this disdain was unconscious. Some was well-hidden, but some leaked out in public utterances and private conversations. On more than one occasion, Sir Tyrone had told eager audiences that his intention was to bring "great drama to an area which has had no theatre." While it was certainly true that the Midwest had never had theatre according to *Guthrie's* definition, it was not always endearing to the community to dismiss so flippantly a long-established professional stock company, a hundred or more well-supported community theatres, and a multitude of dedicated university and high-school theatre people who had labored long and lovingly to create an appetite for theatre in their communities. This faint patronizing created problems in community relations which have never entirely been solved.

Guthrie's solution to the cultural barrenness of the "provinces" was simple and forthright. He cast himself and his cohorts as Three Wise Men from the East bearing the gifts and traditions of British and European theatre which were to be imposed upon the community most willing to accept the imposition. In the beginning, at least, theirs was not an attempt to build a theatre to fit and serve a particular community, but to find a community which would fit and serve a particular theatre—Guthrie's theatre. They had come in quest of audience —an audience ready and willing to accept this predetermined concept of theatre. Their assumption was that, once the unwashed were baptized in the rivers of Guthrie's classical drama, the audience would be saved forever.

As Guthrie states, the Twin Cities seemed like an appropriately small pond in which to be a big fish. But the real basis of the founders' hunch, in our opinion, was that they sensed in the Twin Cities and its immediate area a higher degree of openminded, intellectual curiosity than they had previously found or expected to find anywhere in "the provinces."

Their instinct about the community has ample basis in fact. The Twin Cities, which are basically brain-industry cities, have little geographic reason to grow and prosper. Their vitality stems primarily from the application of creative imagination. The entire region served by the Twin Cities reflects this intellectual strength. It is a highly literate area; Iowa ranks first in the country in literacy. It is a well-educated area: a major university and six liberal arts colleges are located within the Twin Cities. Since World War II the Hormel Meat Packing Company in Austin, Minnesota, has not hired a hog buyer who was not a college graduate, and usually the graduate of a school with an active theatre program. It is an area of openminded people who have produced extremes in politics on both the left and right. It is an area where most people assume you are a "good guy" until you prove otherwise, where people come to the theatre expecting to have fun rather than challenging the performer to entertain them. And, contrary to the Wise Men, it has long been a hotbed of theatre and cultural activity. In fact, according to John K. Sherman in his book *A History of the Arts in Minnesota,* "the honor of originating the little theatre idea in America . . . goes to Duluth, which in November of 1914 organized a community playhouse." Theirs was the first theatre in America to produce Shaw's *Dark Lady of the Sonnets,* and Lady Gregory herself visited Duluth to see the production.

Guthrie, Rea, and Zeisler had sensed this open-minded intellectual curiosity, a characteristic which they believed would give them potential audiences ready and willing to have a go at the type of theatre they proposed. Their hunch proved right, at least in the beginning. We are convinced that the initial box office success of the Minnesota Theatre Company was not due to its promotional efforts; in our opinion, had the same building, staff, and company been set down anywhere else in the United States at that time, it would not have succeeded to the same degree. What made the difference was the fact that in the Midwest, there was an audience which was ready and willing to venture into this kind of dramatic experience; an audience which had already been created by a vast number of circumstances and people, including those who had worked for years in the isolated vineyards of theatre to stimulate a love for the art. There was, indeed, as the triumvirate suspected, an audience curious enough to let a theatre be imposed upon it—at least for a time.

But there remained unanswered a question which was to nag us from the moment we became associated with the company: Can a theatre which has been rigidly imposed upon a community continue to attract audiences after the first surge of curiosity *unless* that theatre is flexible enough to search out, understand, reflect upon, and then serve the needs of that community?

Chapter 2

Six Dollars and
Thirty-Seven Cents

Lou Gelfand opened the door to his office and laughed all over again. It was still something of a shock to see his desk in the middle of a 30 × 50 foot art gallery full of pottery and jade. But that's where the administrator of the new non-profit Tyrone Guthrie Theatre Foundation had his headquarters.

Gelfand's job was to coordinate the monumental fund-raising efforts being made by the finance committee; arrange appearances for Rea and Guthrie; make as many speeches himself as possible; recruit volunteers; get things organized; open the mail. He sat down to perform the latter task.

Things seemed to be going well. The T. B. Walker Foundation grant had given the drive real momentum. Nobody was actually turning down requests for money, and contributions were coming from all over the Midwest—from businessmen, housewives, professional men, corporations, clubs, and school benefits. Yet they were little more than half-way to the goal of $2,300,000, and things were getting tougher. Gelfand wondered if they'd ever actually make it to the end of the road.

The next letter he picked up jingled. He slit the end. Out fell $6.37 with a short note from a Sunday-

*school class in the town of Mankato, Minnesota. An
enormous smile spread across his face. Somehow there
didn't really seem to be too much to worry about.*

That "widow's mite" of $6.37 was one of nearly 8,000 contri-
butions that built the Tyrone Guthrie Theatre, and it was one
of the first indications that the Guthrie-Rea-Zeisler hunch was
right. There *was* an extraordinary open-minded willingness at
the grass roots to find out what this kind of theatre was all
about.

As is normal in such a fund drive, about 90 percent of
the total money raised came from about 10 percent of the
contributors—foundations and corporations. But the funds col-
lected from the more than 7,000 individual contributions is far
from usual, and is not only a remarkable tribute to the community, but also to the efforts of Gelfand, the finance committee (headed by transportation-company president Louis
Zelle), and Guthrie and Rea.

The financial mechanics of the fund-raising drive are not
important to the story of the theatre's eventual audience-
development efforts, but the image presented to the public
during the drive is significant. The public's first impressions
were to have even more and longer-lasting impact upon its
attitude toward buying tickets than upon its donation of funds.
Rea and Guthrie were in the forefront of the efforts to present
the story to the public. Singly and in tandem they attended
coffee parties, luncheons, cocktail hours, cocktail suppers, dinners, afterdinners, school convocations, and church gatherings. They had innumerable private talks with businessmen,
and they filled the air with radio and television interviews. Of
one such concentrated stint, Guthrie writes in *A New Theatre*:
"After only ten days, neither of us ever wished to look a martini
in the face again and had difficulty not making compulsive
recruiting speeches to one another in the men's rooms or as we
sped by taxi from one engagement to the next." Through the
committee's efforts the team toured not only the Twin Cities,
but also hamlets, towns, and villages from one end of Minnesota to the other. They personally presented their message to

thousands, and reached hundreds of thousands more through the coverage given by press, radio, and TV.

Rea and Guthrie sold their product well. Moral support for an idealistic dream is easy to come by; the call for cash support raises questions: "What do I get out of helping you? Why should I buy your product?" The answers were two-fold: (1) Culture (always with a capital *C*) for the community and (2) prestige for the state. Give us a theatre and your support, said Guthrie and Rea, and we will give you great classical drama, excitingly performed, and make your state the home of the greatest repertory theatre in the United States.

As collateral on their promise they offered a professionally-skilled triumvirate: Guthrie (often called the greatest director in the English-speaking world), Rea (an experienced, first-rate manager-producer), and Zeisler (who had excellent, proven professional technical experience).

In theory, selling a triumvirate was sound, for the implications were that the new theatre would exist independently of any one mere mortal. But in actuality it did not work. Rea, charming and witty in his own right, was overshadowed in the public eye by the glamor of a knight of the British Empire. And Peter Zeisler—chained to his desk at the Lunt and Fontanne Theatre in New York, where he was stage-managing *The Sound of Music*—was virtually unknown to the Midwest public in the theatre's formative years. During those fund-raising months the theatre emerged largely as one man—Sir Tyrone Guthrie—and this later proved to be the source of more than one problem in public relations and audience development.

The fund goal was met. The public bought the idea, digging into its pockets out of either civic or intellectual pride—both good reasons. To business organizations and businessmen, the new theatre would be a prestige factor for the community, a talking point in hiring top executives. "See how cultural we are. . . . What a fine city for you to raise your children in." To the aspiring elite, the prospect of the new theatre was a status symbol. "We must live up to our cultural responsibilities." To the theatre-minded intellectuals, the new theatre would bring tangible benefits. "Imagine, the finest classical plays, professionally done, right here where we can see them." And to the Sunday-school class in Mankato—what prompted its outpouring of faith in the form of six dollars and thirty-seven cents? Perhaps it gave simply because the pupils somehow were convinced that their gift would ultimately enhance their future and the future of their children in a very tangible way.

When the drive was over, the general public—the future ticket buyers—was left with the impression of a theatre created because of a desire for community prestige, a theatre which was dominated by a British Knight and which would present Culture. Yet, though the opening battle was won, those first impressions of the Theatre were to become problems in an area vaster by far than the limits of "Good Old Minn."

Chapter 3

Ya Gotta Know
the Territory

*The strains of a fifty-piece amateur orchestra com-
mendably negotiating the score of a Schubert symphony wafted out the doors of a spanking new community center, open to the unseasonable warmth of a
March Sunday in 1965. Inside, the end of the concert
was greeted with enthusiastic applause by the crowd.
This was dedication day for the center, a building
made possible by a $125,000 bequest from a local
farmer and a like amount voted in a bond issue to
provide a facility for the community theatre.*

*A municipal judge introduced the main speaker
of the afternoon: Sir Tyrone Guthrie, who began by
praising the orchestra for a concert he admitted he
expected to be dreadful. Then, with characteristic
charm, he chastised the American public for their low
level of cultural appreciation, blew the golden trumpets for classical theatre, slapped the wrists of the
community for designing a theatre which he called
"this dump," and finally commended them warmly
for the foresight, dedication, and tenacity which it
had taken to bring the building into existence.*

*Their hands still tingling with applause, the
members of the audience followed their pied piper of
Culture to the museum for tea, where Sir Tyrone and*

Lady Guthrie stood in the reception line for an hour conversing, shaking hands, and kissing babies with the skill and aplomb of the best politicians.

It was a day never to be forgotten in Cherokee, Iowa—247 miles southwest of "their" Guthrie Theatre in Minneapolis.

Five years earlier, when he was stumping "Good Old Minn," Tyrone Guthrie would never have believed that someday people as far away as Cherokee, Iowa, or a thousand miles west in Montana would look upon the theatre he was promoting as "their" theatre. Neither he nor his partners were then aware of the unique nature of the geographic area served by Minneapolis and St. Paul, and they had no realization that the theatre would some day be drawing audiences regularly from towns as far west of the Twin Cities as Philadelphia is east. As the vastness of the Twin Cities market area was to have considerable effect on audience development techniques for the Minnesota Theatre Company, some insight into this geographic phenomenon will place many of our activities in proper perspective.

Minneapolis, St. Paul, and the communities within a hundred-mile radius have a combined population of a million and a half. In the rest of the area which focuses upon the Twin Cities the population totals four and a half million—six million in all. It is the only major metropolitan center within a vast, yet cohesive, area which stretches an awesome fifteen hundred miles from the Rocky Mountains east to Eau Claire, Wisconsin; and nearly five hundred miles from Vermillion, South Dakota, and Waterloo, Iowa, north to the Canadian border. It is an incredible four hundred thousand square miles in size—representing more than 10 percent of the nation's land but less than 4 percent of the population. Within the area are located five million acres of state and national parks, mountain peaks soaring up to 12,799 feet, the nation's second largest seaport by tonnage (Duluth), more than 12 percent of the nation's surface water, the geographic center of the United States (in Butte County, South Dakota), 4,772 miles of rivers, and some of the world's richest farming country.

"Here is the land," writes novelist A. B. Guthrie, Jr., "stunning in distance, dizzying to the incredulous eye; and the spirit of the onlooker lifts as he looks and tells himself he must be asleep yet knows he's not."

All of this vast region focuses upon Minneapolis and St. Paul. Through the Twin Cities run all the main arteries of transportation. Here are the headquarters of the Ninth Federal Reserve District which encompasses most of this land. Here is the heart of distribution activity and the center for processing and marketing the area's wealth of agricultural products. Here is the focus of commerce, finance, entertainment, sports, shopping, publishing, broadcasting, and the arts. In Havre, Montana, the Minnesota Twins are "our ball club." From all over the area people come by busload and trainload to support "their team." In Rapid City, South Dakota, football fans loyally follow the Minnesota Vikings. Families in Chippewa Falls, Wisconsin, have charge accounts at Dayton's department store, as do families in Glendive, Montana, and Cedar Falls, Iowa. The businessman, professional man, or farmer in Minot, North Dakota, may typically travel to the Twin Cities half-a-dozen times a year.

This, then, is the nature of the community which the Tyrone Guthrie Theatre was eventually to serve. It was natural that such potential and the geographical vastness should affect *how* we particularly planned and carried out our quest for audience, but this does not make less valid for any theatre the lessons we learned from *what* we did. Every artistic institution serves a community made of many parts but bonded together by common interests and purposes. Audience development should begin with a careful definition of the community. Then action can be planned to fit that community, no matter how small or how large.

By 1962 the theatre's community had contributed over two million dollars; the Tyrone Guthrie Theatre was being built; and the Minnesota Theatre Company Foundation, which was to operate the performing company, was being formed. The time had come to chart a course of action designed to fill the seats for the first season of performances—1,437 seats, eight times a week, for 20 weeks—229,920 seats in all.

Chapter 4

The Morison Report

The executive committee of the Minnesota Theatre Company was gathered around the luncheon table on a sunny October day in 1962 examining a 62-page mimeographed document entitled: "A Plan of Strategy for Promotion, Publicity and Public Relations for the Tyrone Guthrie Theatre, 1963 Season." Brad Morison, then copy chief in the Minneapolis office of Batten, Barton, Durstine and Osborn advertising agency (BBD&O), was explaining page by page the plan which he had volunteered to write.

When the group dutifully reached the bottom of the last page (A Catalogue of Materials), Roger Kennedy, a St. Paul bank executive and the committee's chairman, spoke: "I move that the Washburn Report be adopted as the plan of strategy for 1963."

There were puzzled expressions around the table but, long overdue at their desks, the members of the committee quickly voted "aye." It was so entered in the minutes. The "Washburn Report" was to be the official bible of audience-development efforts in that first season. It was several weeks later when Oliver Rea finally got the answer to the question that had puzzled the committee. "Just out of curiosity," he

> asked Kennedy the next time they met, "why did you
> call that the Washburn report?"
>
> "Because," answered Kennedy, "it was written by
> Brad Washburn, wasn't it?"
>
> The plan of strategy for the Minnesota Theatre
> Company had been indelibly named for a prominent
> Minnesota Republican—the wrong Brad.

The Morison Report was the first of continuing attempts by the
Public Relations Department of the Minnesota Theatre Company to apply basic and accepted techniques of marketing to
the problems of promoting a theatre. Yet since *sell* is a four-
letter word, it seems to be considered a dirty one to many people in the arts. There were many strenuous but sincere objec-
tions during our tenure to efforts to run even one phase of the
theatre's operations like a business. After four years of experience, we still can find no valid reasons why proven marketing
techniques should *not* be applied to the development of audience for the arts. Rather, in view of their growing economic
plight, there seem to be imperative reasons why businesslike
methods *must* be used. But it should be done with the understanding of several basic principles.

    1. No amount of promotion, no matter how creative, can
"sell" a bad product. Such efforts will only hasten failure.
Therefore, the primary prerequisite to enthusiastic public acceptance of a product, service, or idea is the creation of something that fills a genuine need.

    2. There is one fundamental difference between selling a
product in the commercial market place and selling an artistic
institution. If the public does not like a commercial product,
there is freedom to change the product to suit public demand.
In the arts the product is based on an artistic philosophy. The
people charged with the responsibility to sell this product have
no right to suggest changes in philosophy to please the public;
they have only the challenge to educate that public to appreciate the philosophy.

    3. The basic aim of marketing is efficiency of communica-
tion through selectivity. There are few products needed by

everyone. It is therefore inefficient, wasteful, and almost impossible to try to communicate regularly with *all* of the people. Marketing techniques *attempt to define* which groups of people are most likely to be prospects, what to say, how to say it effectively, and how to reach the selected groups of people efficiently. The Morison Report was an attempt to define by geographic, demographic, and psychological characteristics those people who would probably be most receptive to the Minnesota Theatre Company story, and then to try to determine the most effective and efficient ways of reaching those people.

The business world has long accepted the necessity of facts for effective marketing, and enormous sums of money go toward identifying prospects and determining their attitudes and needs. Unfortunately, there is not a similar body of knowledge regarding the arts. A search revealed that, aside from one survey of audience made by the Minneapolis Symphony Orchestra in 1956, there was no factual information in existence about the cultural habits and attitudes of people in the area. The most meaningful source of information seemed to be the list of people who attended spring performances of the Metropolitan Opera in the Twin Cities, because the Metropolitan drew from the same geographical area from which the theatre hoped to draw. The market-analysis section of the Morison Report was based on a detailed analysis of the opera audience, plus some calculated guesswork and carefully considered assumptions based on 15 years' experience in advertising and communications. It was a patchwork job which would have been totally unacceptable to a sophisticated advertising client because of its lack of background research. But it was a starting point. It set goals and outlined methods for trying to reach them. Most importantly it helped to reduce wasted effort because it pinpointed tasks to reach a defined objective rather than suggesting approaches always tried in the theatre.

Many of the original premises of the report were substantially revised as we went along. Others were embraced even more wholeheartedly than when first proposed. From this point, we will use the report as a foundation for this book. We will outline the points of the original strategy and then attempt to show how they proved valid or invalid, where we succeeded or failed, and how broader concepts of those strategies became apparent to us. Most importantly, however, we will attempt to set forth the questions which have arisen in our minds concerning our initial premises and the generally accepted practices of audience development.

One lesson became evident on September 20, 1963: That even a little bit of patchwork market analysis can be remarkably helpful and accurate. The Morison Report, with its free-wheeling predictions, had forecast a total first-season audience of 181,220. The final statement for the 1963 season read: "Total Paid Attendance at Public Performances, 183,981."

Part Two

Market Analysis and Research

If we could first know where we are and whither we are tending, we could better judge what we do and how to do it.

ABRAHAM LINCOLN

Chapter 5

First Guesses

In the wee hours of a September morning in 1962 Anne Richards sat at a desk in her apartment laboriously computing the sales breakdown of Metropolitan Opera tickets in towns 76 to 100 miles from the Twin Cities. She was to become public relations assistant with the Minnesota Theatre Company, but at the moment she was a BBD&O secretary, and somewhat disenchanted with the fact that she had volunteered to help Morison analyze potential audience for his report. The figures, as they had been all day, were falling into a monotonous pattern. Waseca, Minnesota: 69.4 tickets per 10,000 population; New Ulm: 58.5; Clara City: 53.3; Barron, Wisconsin: 70.0.

Suddenly she shook her head in disbelief. A town of fewer than 2,000 had opera ticket sales of 382.0 per 10,000 population. She tried again. Same answer. She could hardly contain her curiosity until the next morning.

By the beginning of the business day she had the editor of the town's newspaper on the telephone. "Was there any special reason," she asked, "why so many people there went to the opera?"

"Well, there's this one woman in town," said the editor. "She's nutty about opera and she's rich. So she *buys a lot of tickets and gives them away to a lot of different folks around here. But I'm not sure anybody ever uses them."*

Despite some wild variations traceable to local idiosyncrasies, the Metropolitan Opera ticket-sales figures proved invaluable in the initial market analysis. The object of this analysis was to locate the potential audience geographically in order to use our time and effort most efficiently. We also hoped for statistical benchmarks of cultural interest in every town, against which we could eventually measure the success of promotional efforts. The sales per ten thousand population of opera tickets was computed for every town in six states and plotted on a graph against distance from the Twin Cities (see Appendix, Figure 1). The curve started high, took a drastic nosedive at a distance of about a hundred miles, and then leveled out and became virtually flat after three hundred miles. From this, two conclusions could be drawn:

1. When people had to travel more than one hundred miles, they attended with considerably less frequency. Apparently a hundred miles was as far as they could or would go for entertainment and return home the same night.
2. There was a certain nucleus of people who would travel to the Twin Cities for the opera *no matter how far* they had to come.

These two conclusions led to two assumptions:

1. The theatre's area of primary potential lay within a one-hundred-mile radius of the Twin Cities. (This was logically the *only* area of potential for season tickets, since it was unrealistic to expect people to plan several different overnight trips months in advance.)
2. The theatre probably could count on some dedicated support from even beyond this area.

From the opera statistics and other data we could arrange the rest of the territory according to potential. The people within the one-hundred-mile radius were designated Group I (see Appendix, Figure 2). Surrounding the Group I area and extending as far as five hundred miles to the north and west were some three million people who naturally gravitated toward the Twin Cities; these were designated Group IIA. Still further to the north and west were another two million people just as naturally oriented toward the Twin Cities but, because of distance, less frequent visitors; this was labelled Group IIB. To the south and east—in Iowa, Wisconsin, Illinois, Nebraska, and Missouri—was an area from which the Minnesota lake country drew most of its summer visitors. For business and shopping they gravitated toward other metropolitan areas—Chicago, Des Moines, Omaha, Kansas City, Milwaukee. But some six hundred and fifty thousand of this nearly 14 million population funneled through the Twin Cities according to 1962 statistics from the Minnesota Department of Business Development. These people were designated as Group III in the breakdown of potential audience. Group IV was everybody else in the United States, but specifically the one hundred and thirty thousand people who traveled to the Twin Cities for business or recreational purposes (see Appendix, Figure 2).

Our potential audience was now defined geographically in terms of the probability of their attending; we could begin to organize our efforts for maximum efficiency. The press list, for example, was broken down by these geographic groupings so that we could send more releases and pictures where it would do the most good and tailor releases to the habits of the people in the areas. We were also now in a position to estimate the first year's attendance, but first a vital question had to be answered. How closely would the appeal of grand opera and the theatre's productions parallel each other? The Metropolitan played one week in May to standing-room-only houses. The Minnesota Theatre Company was to play twenty weeks in summer and early fall. But theoretically, grand opera has less general appeal than serious theatre.

Opera-ticket sales were compared with what little information was available on theatre-ticket sales and we guessed that *four times as many people would be interested in the type of theatre the company planned to present as were interested in grand opera*. (The factor of four eventually proved to be wrong. It turned out to be six.) Using this factor we then made the following estimates of total potential audience for 1963:

Estimated Audience Potential based on
Opera Ticket Sales

Group I (100-mile area)
        Population: 1,540,000
        Opera tickets per 10M: 150
        Potential MTC attendance: 154 × 150 × 4   92,400

Group IIA (500-mile area)
        Population: 3,336,000
        Opera tickets per 10M: 25.0
        Potential MTC attendance: 333.6 × 25 × 4   33,360

Group IIB (Balance of Region)
        Population: 2,188,796
        Opera tickets per 10M: 10.0
        Potential MTC attendance: 218.8 × 10 × 4   8,720

Group III (Summer visitors)
        Population passing through Twin Cities: 650,000
        Since they are IN the Twin Cities, potential
        assumed to be the same as Group I: 150
        Potential MTC audience: 65 × 150 × 4   39,000

Group IV (others)
        Population coming to Twin Cities: 130,000
        Potential again assumed the same as Group I: 150
        Potential MTC audience: 13 × 150 × 4   7,800

                                        TOTAL   181,220

Reduced to percentages, the estimated audience for the first season was, geographically:

Group I	(100-mile area)	51 percent
Group IIA	(500-mile area)	19
Group IIB	(balance of region)	5
Group III	(summer visitors)	21
Group IV	(others)	4

Now our course was more definite. Until more accurate information was available, these were the proportions in which the public relations department's time, energy, and money should be expended.

The detailed accounting of this statistical analysis is not meant to suggest that the actual figures are pertinent to any other theatre in any other location. Rather, it is meant to illustrate how such an analysis can be done to help direct promotional efforts toward areas of prime potential. There is no community, whether it is a selected portion of a small metropolitan area or an enormous geographic entity, which cannot similarily be dissected so that limited resources can be channeled more efficiently. For any artistic institution, a breakdown of ticket sales by postal zone or census tract could be extremely helpful. Such figures, when compared with census data on the socioeconomic level of the population in each area, would give an invaluable indication of weak areas where additional efforts should be made.

Without any previous attendance statistics, we were forced in the beginning to let our efforts be guided by the Morison Report's patchwork market analysis. But soon there would be live audiences attending live performances. Our next job was to find out as much about those audiences as we could.

Chapter 6

The Moment of Truth

Oliver Rea raised the blinds of his office on a dazzling May day and sat down at his rolltop desk. The young company had its first two openings out of the way and was smoothly settling down to the repertory of Hamlet *and* The Miser.

Rea had just begun to open his mail when the spring calm was shattered by a thunderous knock on the door, followed immediately by associate artistic director Douglas Campbell, clutching a small folder.

"Oliver, this is outrageous!" Campbell began.

"Oh, don't you like it?" Rea hedged. "I thought it was rather handsome, myself."

"No, I don't mean the way it looks," Campbell roared. "I mean asking people who come to the theatre to fill out some kind of a bloody form. They come to be entertained, not to answer a bunch of silly questions."

Rea began an explanation of the need for information on who was attending the theatre, but Campbell wasn't in a listening mood.

"You Americans are all alike," he stormed. "This question about 'how are you enjoying the performance?' Why, an actor knows that by instinct! And the

> *question about occupation. I can tell by walking into*
> *the lobby who's attending the performance."*
>
> *Rea parried. "Can you tell whether they're from*
> *North Dakota, or Iowa?" he asked.*
>
> *Campbell slowed down. "What possible difference*
> *does that make?"*
>
> *"It makes the difference," Rea said, "in whether*
> *you travel north, west, or south to tell people what*
> *they're missing."*

When the Minnesota Theatre Company played its first performance, neither Douglas Campbell nor Tyrone Guthrie had seen the Morison Report. It is doubtful even that either of them has ever seen it, since Rea probably felt it more judicious to keep it well hidden from two men who believe instinct is the most satisfactory fuel on which to run a theatre. If either had read it, it is conceivable that he would have resoundingly vetoed a recommendation for "a brief questionnaire designed by a research expert which every person attending every performance of the theatre would be asked to fill out concerning where they came from, why they were in Minneapolis, and how they heard about the Guthrie Theatre." But since 20,000 questionnaires had already been printed by May 7, 1963, the opposition retreated and the analysis of the first season's audience proceeded.

The reason for the research is evident: to check the accuracy of the guesses in the Morison Report and to find out whom we had reached with the theatre's story in terms of age, sex, geographical location of home, occupation, education, and other data. Even more important, we hoped to discover those whom we had *not* reached so that we could go to work on them the following season.

Under the guidance of BBD&O research director Richard Rundle, the structure of the research changed slightly from the original recommendation. A printed folder (see Appendix, Figure 3) with 11 questions and a pencil was inserted in every tenth program at every performance during the 20-week season. Boxes were placed in the lobbies to collect the questionnaires.

Apparently the public did not feel as outraged by the questionnaire as did Campbell, for the response was excellent. Fifty percent of the questionnaires were returned, giving a study sample of 10,421—a remarkable return in this kind of sampling procedure. Some questions which could be verified by fact (for example, the number of season tickets versus single tickets sold) showed that the sample was an amazingly accurate cross-section of the total audience.

The results of the survey—which cost about $1,900— were fascinating and invaluable (see Table 1 in Appendix). In some cases, they led us to direct and immediate action. Other uses of the results are less measurable because everyone in the public relations department became so steeped in knowledge of the audience that they unconsciously applied it to almost everything they did.

It should plainly be stated, however, that we failed to take action in many areas where the audience study clearly called for it. A more concentrated effort should have been made, for instance, to reach the engineers, technical workers, sales clerks, and clerical and secretarial workers. Some of the blame for our neglect in these areas can be placed on the lack of time and money, some on lack of insight as to what to do. Either way, we failed to exploit completely the wealth of knowledge which the survey revealed. But at least now we had facts to give us direction and we could go to work. The next question: Was the work paying off?

It would take another book to delve into the significance of all the data uncovered, which was tabulated in many ways. We were able, for instance, to study the difference in the characteristics of people who bought tickets for $1.50 as opposed to those who purchased the $5 seats. However, our initial interest was in the geographic distribution of audience. The results as compared with the Morison Report estimates are shown in the accompanying table on page 29.

We had clearly underestimated potential within the Group I area. The interest in theatre within this group was not four times as great as in opera, but six times. There was no reason to believe that the interest factor was not as valid in Groups II and III as in Group I, so we had fallen even further short of

Comparison of 1963 Audience Study with
Morison Report Estimates

	Estimate of Potential		Actual Attendance (1963)	
Group I	92,400	51 percent	139,913	77.3 percent
Group II	42,080	24	11,946	6.6
Group III	39,000	21	13,937	7.7
Group IV	7,800	4	17,135	8.4

reaching the potential in those areas than the figures indicated. The reason probably was that we had done a much better job of communicating information about the theatre in Group I than elsewhere. There was enormous untapped potential in Groups II and III—close to 100,000 in excellent potential attendance over and above what the theatre had attracted that first season. From that point on there was a very definite shift of time, effort, and money in the direction of increased communication in Iowa, Wisconsin, and the Dakotas. The effort began by assigning a staff member to each state with instructions to travel, to study the state, to get to know its people, and to determine the best way to communicate information about the theatre in these areas.

The study also yielded helpful information about attendance from within Group I. The audience from Minneapolis and its suburbs was 3.27 times as large as that from St. Paul and its suburbs; yet the Minneapolis population is only double that of St. Paul. We had missed our mark in St. Paul, and began to take immediate steps to fortify the theatre's position there. We started by substantially increasing the number of volunteers in Minneapolis' sister city for the 1964 season ticket drive.

Elsewhere in Group I, using data from the study and the theatre's list of ticket buyers, we computed sales per ten thousand population for the first season and compared them with the comparable statistics for opera tickets. A list was made of the ten major towns where the theatre was strongest in relation to opera sales. Assignment: Find out why the theatre did so well. A list was made of the ten major towns which were weakest in comparison. Assignment: Exert more effort.

Demographically the figures were equally revealing. The theatre's audience was highly educated (19.2 percent had some college, 28.9 percent had bachelor's degrees, 32.7 percent had advanced degrees); fairly well spread in age range (5.7 percent were under 18, 17.8 percent were from 18 to 25, 25.7 percent were 26 to 35, 27.3 percent were 36 to 49, 23.4 percent were 50 or over); high in the professionally employed (39.5 percent of men, 23.5 percent of women, 31.2 percent all respondents); and extremely low in sales-clerk, clerical, or secretarial job classifications (4.7 percent), engineers and technical workers (3.7 percent), and blue-collar workers (3.1 percent). We assumed at the time that this was probably fairly typical of performing-arts audiences, an assumption which was recently proved valid by the audience analysis contained in the Twentieth Century Fund Study, *Performing Arts: The Economic Dilemma*.[1] (A comparison of the two studies is included in the Appendix in Table 2.)

But just because the audience was typical did not mean to us that it could not be changed. It seemed logical that we should at least attempt to develop programs which would increase audience within a certain age group or occupation where there appeared to be potential. The research findings gave us some broad goals:

1. With half of the nation's population now under 25 years of age, it seemed logical that we should try to put more accent on youth to increase that portion of the audience.

2. In 1963 the theatre had sold 8,507 tickets to women who classified themselves as having sales-clerk, clerical, or secretarial positions. Allowing for multiple-ticket purchases, probably only about 5,000 different people had been reached in this category, yet in Minneapolis alone there are more than 8,000 such people. A prime target.

3. With industries such as Honeywell, 3M Company and Control Data so important in the Twin Cities, the 3.7 percent of the audience composed of engineers and technical workers seemed an extremely low figure and one that could well be increased.

Thus, although the Morison Report had enabled us to set certain potential goals, the 1963 Analysis of Audience told us

[1] *William J. Baumol and William G. Bowen,* Performing Arts: The Economic Dilemma, *New York, Twentieth Century Fund, 1966.*

of the strengths and weaknesses in our efforts with respect to those goals. The importance of working from such knowledge cannot be overemphasized. Without these two studies there would have been no way of knowing that in the first season we had completely missed close to one hundred thousand potential attendance in Groups II and III, and our promotional efforts probably would have remained haphazard and ineffectual in those areas.

Chapter 7

Continuing Research

Twenty-six ladies pulled their wooden folding chairs into a semi-circle in the rather gloomy basement of a church in a small Minnesota town some distance from the Twin Cities. Soon they were relaxed and chatting freely in answer to questions about their families' entertainment habits put to them by three members of the theatre's staff. It was five months until the theatre would open.

This was what BBD&O calls a "focus group"—a small group of people randomly gathered together to help give focus to questions later used in quantitative research.

As the dialogue continued, Morison became aware that very few of the women seemed to travel to the Twin Cities with any frequency, if at all. He could see the props being knocked out from under some of the basic assumptions of the Morison Report. When the opportunity presented itself, he took aside the woman who had assembled the group. Was this typical, he asked, of the people in this particular town? "Oh, goodness, no," she said blithely. "You see, about half these ladies are from the state mental hospital and they don't get around very much."

There are those wags who might suggest that the group assembled in the church basement that gray November day of 1962 was the ideal one with which to conduct theatre research. But the findings of that particular day were rather hastily abandoned and we chose another town for our pilot research!

Later audience research would be grander and more accurate, but this early group research was useful and, as proven later, valid. The focus-group research gave us personal rather than statistical insight on the theatre's image. It also gave us a means of determining trends and attitudes of the public by reinterviewing at the end of the season.

The Morison Report had recommended that nine towns be set up as "pilot-research towns" for long-range and continuing research. The plan was to do some immediate research in each town, aimed at verifying or refuting some of the assumptions used in the market analysis. In addition, we hoped to learn more about communicating with prospective theatre-goers, and to determine their knowledge of the Tyrone Guthrie Theatre. With these preopening benchmarks, the pilot towns could then become valuable bases for continuing research through the years.

The towns selected were to be typical of those in Group I, Group IIA, Group IIB, and Group III. The research was to be conducted in the following way: A church women's group in each city was to be asked to assemble a group of some 25 women who were typical of the town. Someone from the theatre would meet with them for an hour to chat informally about their entertainment and travel habits. On the basis of this information, and the feel of the city gained from the experience, a questionnaire would be designed. The women's group would be paid 25 cents per call to telephone persons picked at random from the town telephone book and to complete the questionnaires. (Both the focus-group technique and the system of paying church women's groups for telephone interviews are excellent ways of obtaining information inexpensively, and, in many situations, can be used to great advantage by cultural organizations.)

Because of a lack of staff time, the pilot-research town plan was carried out in only one of the nine cities—Little Falls,

Minnesota, a town of about 7,500 population situated 100 miles from the Twin Cities. The results were interesting, although not nearly as valuable as if there had been eight other cities for comparison. For example, the findings from this study were our first indication that the 4:1 opera-interest ratio we had set up was too low. The validity of the 100-mile radius for Group I was bolstered by the town research, which also indicated a rather remarkable awareness (70 percent) of the Guthrie Theatre six months before its doors were opened. The telephone interviews also told us something about the theatre's image. In response to a question asking him to describe briefly his impressions of the Tyrone Guthrie Theatre, one man answered: "They're going to go in for heavy drama." His answer was typical.

At the end of the first season in December, 1963, we returned to Little Falls to measure our success. Awareness of the theatre had jumped from 70 percent of those interviewed in 1962 to 99 percent, while "knowledgeability" jumped from 21 to 65 percent of those interviewed. About 25 percent of the interviewees said they had attended a play at the Guthrie Theatre, and 48 percent said they planned or hoped to attend the following year. (It should be pointed out that such random-sampling figures are most valuable when compared with each other—or with previous, comparable figures—rather than with available factual data such as population.)

Of those who did attend a play in 1963, 80 percent said they hoped to, or definitely would, attend a production in 1964. But this left 20 percent of those who had attended who were *not* planning to return the next season. We would have to continue promotional work to bring back this 20 percent of the audience.

In retrospect, it seems that we would have been wise to carry out the pilot-research program in its entirety. It might have helped to correct some of the assumptions of the original report, and it would have given us an excellent preopening benchmark against which we could have continued to check our success—or failure—in communicating with the public.

Although the pilot town program was not carried out as proposed, we continued to use various research and research techniques to substitute knowledge for guesswork whenever possible. When, early in 1964, we decided to launch a limited campaign to capture the sales clerk, clerical, and secretarial job categories, we began with a small focus group of working girls. On the basis of what the girls told us, a questionnaire was composed and distributed to a large sampling of girls in the appropriate categories. The results led us to seek the cooperation of several restaurants, hotels, and department stores in setting up "clubs" or "special theatre dinners" for the business girl. (The events were given adequate promotion and good business cooperation, but even so, they were not as successful as we had hoped.)

Also, in 1964, a questionnaire was distributed to the audience, asking for their preferences of performance days and times. The results led directly to changing curtain times from 8:30 P.M. to 8 P.M., and from 2:00 P.M. to 1:30 P.M., and changing from a Monday-evening to a Sunday-afternoon performance.

In the summer of 1966, when it became apparent that the Minnesota Theatre Company would probably be performing a season in St. Paul in addition to the Minneapolis season, a research project was initiated to determine attitudes of theatregoers in each city about their habits in traveling city-to-city for entertainment. Ten women from the theatre's women's volunteer organization, called The Stagehands, were trained in interviewing techniques by a BBD&O research staff member. Each volunteer was assigned 10 depth interviews carefully chosen to cover areas of known theatre interest in St. Paul and Minneapolis. The resulting information was analyzed to help estimate the size of the potential audience for the proposed St. Paul season, and to help structure the most attractive season-ticket and promotional plans for the double season.

Another source of valuable continuing data was the mailing list. At the end of the 1964 season, the list was updated and transferred from cards to magnetic tape. With this new system, the names of season-ticket buyers and single mail-order-ticket buyers, as well as of The Stagehands and the contributors, were stored complete with ticket-buying history since 1963 plus zip-code designation. This system has given us quick access to statistics which might otherwise require days of tedious labor to extract. It enabled us, for instance, to compute very easily 1964 ticket sales by zip zone for the Twin Cities and suburbs. The data were used for the 1965 season-ticket drive to guide The Stagehands toward weak areas where additional volunteers and increased energy were needed. By comparison, in 1966 we were able to tell if efforts in this direction had been successful. (Substantially, they were not.)

The most valuable use of continuing research has been to measure the ways in which the theatre's audience changes, in an attempt to assess the results of our promotional efforts. Was the theatre attracting more people from Groups II and III through the public relations department's extra efforts? Was there increasing attendance from St. Paul in proportion to Minneapolis? Was the audience getting younger? Were more working girls and more engineers being reached?

The budget, ample as it was, did not permit a full-scale audience analysis every season, but in 1964 and 1966 we inserted questionnaires in every tenth program for a period of three weeks in late August and early September, compared the results with the same weeks in 1963, and made projections from the comparison. The results were interesting and valuable. They showed that, almost without exception, the extra efforts had paid off, though not as well in some cases as in others. The geographical comparison is presented in the first of the accompanying tables, while the breakdown between Minneapolis and St. Paul is shown in the second table.

Comparison of Audience Statistics with Estimates of the Morison Report

	1962 Estimate of Potential percent		1963 Attendance percent		1964 Attendance percent		1966 Attendance percent	
Group I	92,400	51	139,913	77.3	142,514	66.4	143,441	67.0
Group II	42,080	24	11,946	6.6	16,097	7.5	16,910	7.9
Group III	39,000	21	13,937	7.7	27,687	12.9	33,184	15.5
Group IV	7,800	4	17,135	8.4	28,332	13.2	20,557	9.6

Audience Statistics for Minneapolis and
St. Paul, 1966 vs. 1963

	1963		*1966*	
Minneapolis	92,563	52.5 percent	87,777	41.0 percent
St. Paul	28,325	15.4	33,826	15.8
Ratio	3.3		2.6	

The most gratifying trend in the figures was the steady
and substantial growth in the audience over four years from
the Group III area, an increase of two and a half times (a total
number approaching the original estimate of audience potential). There was also a growth in Group II, which was less dramatic for a valid reason. Our plan to have a staff member explore thoroughly the surrounding states to determine the best
way to reach that audience never fully materialized. Due to the
lack of time and some personnel changes, North Dakota and
much of South Dakota were not covered. Iowa, Wisconsin,
northern Illinois, and eastern Nebraska, on the other hand,
were rather thoroughly explored and given extra promotional
efforts far in excess of what had been done in the Dakotas. The
results proved such efforts worthwhile.

St. Paul showed a small increase over four years, while
Minneapolis dropped slightly. The ratio between attendance for
the two was coming closer to the ratio of population. It was
evident that attendance from Minneapolis and its suburbs had
remained relatively constant, with small gains in St. Paul, its
suburbs, and towns outside the Twin Cities but within the one-
hundred-mile radius giving slight overall growth to Group I.
Group II showed a small, steady growth and Group III a larger
one, with Group IV fluctuating rather drastically.

The main problem at the moment seemed to be Minneapolis. Did the theatre initially attract nearly all the readily
available potential? Should the theatre now drastically change
its promotional tactics in Minneapolis to prod interest in the
less readily available potential?

Having made the geographic comparison, we could then

explore the audience demographically. Some changes were immediately apparent. A comparative table is shown. The audience was getting slightly younger. The number of men was increasing slightly, maybe because more women were able to talk their husbands into attending with them. There was a small increase in the "engineer–technical" and "sales clerk–clerical –secretarial" categories where we had been putting some, though inadequate, effort. But there had been no increase in businessmen attending.

Comparison of Demographic Characteristics of Minnesota Theatre Company Audiences, 1966 vs. 1963

		1963 percent	*1966 percent*
Age:			
	Under 18	5.7	4.7
	18–25	17.8	23.2
	26–35	25.7	23.2
	36–49	27.3	24.8
	50 or over	23.4	23.8
Sex:			
	Female	55.4	51.2
	Male	44.6	48.8
Occupation:			
	Professional	31.2	29.8
	Housewife	22.9	19.3
	Student	17.9	23.4
	Business	12.8	10.7
	Sales clerk/clerical/secretarial	4.7	5.7
	Technical/engineering	3.7	4.7
	Retired	3.6	2.2
	Blue collar	3.1	3.6

Could the theatre continue to attract a younger audience? Could the theatre effectively devote more time and money toward special occupational groups? Could we find ways to develop a blue-collar audience?

The answers to questions that research poses are not easy to find. But the questions cannot even be asked without the basic knowledge that continuing research provides.

Chapter 8

How Much Is Enough?

"All right, then, why don't you take a poll of your audience on what plays they'd like to see before you ever announce a season?"

The dinner-table argument waxed hot and heavy as a group of professional theatre people from around the country, gathered for a conference, discussed the merits of research in theatre. The speaker was a particularly vehement director.

"Pretty soon you'll have everything on IBM cards and then a computer can direct the plays."

The director's particular targets were Rea and Morison, who had been asked to explain the research program being carried on by the Minnesota Theatre Company. Patiently, but somewhat gropingly, Rea tried to explain the difference between artistic and administrative decisions and the part research should or should not play in each case. Finally a cooler head posed an intriguing and pertinent question.

"Suppose," he said, "you had done a thorough market-research study on each of the cities you visited before you decided on the Twin Cities. What do you think the results would have been?"

Rea slowly lit one of his French cigarettes as he contemplated his answer. Finally he spoke. "My hunch

*is that we would probably have gone to some other
city," he answered. "And I think we probably would
have been wrong."*

It is fascinating to speculate on what the results might have
been if Guthrie, Rea, and Zeisler had commissioned a marketing firm to do studies of potential audience in all of the cities
they considered. Would the studies have confirmed Guthrie's
hunch about Old Minn? Or would the theatre have ended up in
Detroit or Milwaukee or San Francisco? And how would it have
fared? The question of how much part research should play in
the making of major decisions is a ticklish one for any organization, but doubly so for an artistic institution. American business and industry rely heavily upon facts in areas of product
development, marketing, and distribution, but occasionally re-
discover that research is not the whole answer. Ask the man
who bought an Edsel. The battle of research versus creative
instinct is fought daily on Madison Avenue, Wall Street, and
Broadway.

The answer to the question, from our experience, would
seem to relate to the fine line between artistic and administrative decision. Choosing a play obviously should be an artistic
decision, and not one based on research. A director chooses a
particular play because his instinct tells him it is the correct
time and place to do the play with his concept. The audience
can never know until it experiences the performance whether
that play will be important and meaningful, because it cannot
anticipate the director's concept. An audience which said "No"
in advance to *Hamlet* in a research approach to choosing a repertory might be deprived of a *Hamlet* that would have moved
them enormously in performance.

Even choosing a location for the creation of the Guthrie
Theatre may have been, in reality, closer to a pure artistic decision than an administrative one. The theatre, the company,
and the performances were a concept, not a reality, and a concept which could not really be communicated. "Would you support a professional classic repertory company?" is a question
which would get only meaningless answers until the person
queried could experience this particular concept of profes-

sional classic repertory company. It probably had to be Dr. Guthrie who said "This is the right place," because only he could sense the fact that these were the right kind of people to accept what he had in mind.

But, as we move across the no-man's land from artistic to administrative decision, the use of research and fact becomes less frightening and more desirable. In our view, research is imperative in a world of sophisticated communications techniques and vicious competition for the time, mind, and money of man. Without the data to isolate potential and to be selective in communication, more time and money will be wasted than used wisely. No theatre is in a position to waste money. Decades ago, John Wanamaker said, "I know that half of my advertising money is wasted. The trouble is, I don't know which half." Knowledge gleaned from research, testing, and interpretation of existing data is the modern tool we used to keep such waste to a minimum.

One obstacle to better use of research in the arts is that few administrators or public relations people in the field have any knowledge, understanding, or appreciation of the world of facts and figures. People in administrative work in theatre around the country generally do not seem to have the training, experience, or sometimes the desire to grasp the implications or importance of research. In some cases, our enthusiasm for analytical processes has barely been tolerated by friends in the theatre as an idiosyncrasy of two people from the world "outside theatre." Partly, the opposition is a failure to understand the difference between artistic and administrative decision—a failure to understand that the former can be made on a basis of instinct, taste, and opinion while the latter can and must be made from factual knowledge.

Our four years of experience confirmed our belief that research and the tools of market analysis can be of enormous value in the field of audience development. We know that we could have made them even more valuable to the Minnesota Theatre Company if we had had more time and experience. Nor did our four years give us all the answers. We still ask certain questions:

1. How much effect should marketing research have on the establishment or expansion of a theatre? Can public support be predicted accurately in advance? What dangers lie in looking to research for guidance in decisionmaking?

2. How can theatres locate, interpret, and make use of existing research and data? Are today's administrators equipped by training, experience, or temperament to understand, appreciate, and use marketing and research data? If not, how can they be better prepared in this area? Should boards of directors be more insistent that modern marketing practices be followed?

3. Is it possible that some national organization should be collecting, interpreting, and distributing marketing information and supplying professional research counseling to artistic institutions?

Part Three

Psychological Factors and a Strategy

In addition to classifying potential audience by geography and travel habits, it seems obvious that it can be broken down with regard to attitudes toward theatre of this type which can lead to a guiding philosophy by which this theatre will be sold.

The Morison Report

Chapter 9

The Yeses, Maybes, and Noes

A city sight-seeing bus turned away from the sun-streaked green of Minneapolis' Loring Park and headed west past a carefully groomed park garden. Mrs. Lucia Lewis, travel editor for the Chicago Daily News, *was doing a feature on the Twin Cities and had joined the bus-load of tourists for a narrated tour that summer of 1964. The driver's voice rasped over the public address system.*

"On your left, across the beautiful formal garden, you see the Walker Art Center. Next to it is the Tyrone Guthrie Theatre, opened just about a year ago. It is built so that no seat is more than 50 feet from the stage."

There was no further comment. It could have been a movie house or any ordinary theatre. Finally, a curious tourist asked who Tyrone Guthrie was.

"Well," said the driver, "I don't exactly remember whether he was a lumber tycoon or one of our railroad pioneers. Now on your right. . . ."

After a year and a half of performances and nearly three years of rather extraordinary amounts of publicity, a sight-seeing bus driver in Minneapolis was still confusing one of the most distinguished directors in English-speaking theatre with T. B.

Walker, a lumber tycoon whose foundation had contributed land and $500,000 to the Guthrie Theatre. Nor was the driver alone in his confusion and lack of knowledge. It is evident even today from research, observation, and conversations in back-street cafés and suburban country clubs that the vast majority of the population in the theatre's primary area care little about the Minnesota Theatre Company and know less. (It should be noted, however, that shortly after Mrs. Lewis reported the above incident in her newspaper, the sight-seeing bus drivers of the Twin Cities were invited for a performance, a backstage tour, and a brief lecture on the history of the theatre, complete with biographical notes on Sir Tyrone.)

The bus driver and his hundreds of thousands of compatriots who have found even *reading* about the Tyrone Guthrie Theatre uninteresting were what the Morison Report classified as "Type #3 Prospects—People who are quite positive that they do not and will not like classical theatre or anything which has to do with culture or art."

After attempting to identify geographic areas of prime potential, the report then tried using common sense to classify prospective theatre-goers with respect to their attitudes about serious drama. It was necessary to know not only *where* the prospects lived so they could be reached, but *what they thought* about theatre so the right approach could be used. Unfortunately, there was no existing knowledge or research on which to draw for the psychological analysis. It was mostly hunch. The report cavalierly found and described three types of people as follows:

> Type #1—People who *know* they like classical theatre and culture for its own sake, or because their attendance at such events gives them intellectual and/or social status.
> Type #2—People who are uncertain about whether they like or would like classical theatre or things on a so-called "cultural level" and are not driven by the social status urge.
> Type #3—People who are quite positive that they do not and will not like classical theatre or anything which has to do with culture or art.

These types have since become known in the department's vocabulary as the Yeses, Maybes, and Noes. Their identification served as a basis for the general selling and promotion strategy outlined in the next chapter. In 1962 we knew little about these groups with respect either to the *numbers* in which they existed in the area or what *kind* of people demographically comprised each group. Subsequently, we learned more about them, and formulated some interesting theories, which may be helpful to those developing audiences for the arts.

The major portion of Yeses is probably made up of people who buy season tickets. In 1963, the theatre's season-ticket total represented about 1.5 percent of the total population in the geographic Group I area. In 1966, it was exactly one percent. Taking into account those who had bought season tickets only once or twice, it would be safe to figure that the Yeses in the theatre's Group I population of one and a half million probably number about three percent.

The Maybes cannot be estimated as accurately. In 1966 the Minnesota Theatre Company played to a total number of different people from Group I representing about 4 percent of that population. Eliminating the one percent who were season-ticket holders, or Yeses, 3 percent of the Group I population saw one or more plays on a single-ticket basis. This three percent is part, but not all, of the Maybe population. Over four years, the company played to a total number of different people on a single-ticket basis representing about 5 percent of the Group I population. Add to this the season ticket holders and it appears from 7 to 8 percent of the total Group I population had attended the theatre at least once. The Minneapolis *Star* Metro-Poll, taken in the Twin Cities metropolitan area in 1965, showed that 9 percent of those interviewed had attended the Guthrie Theatre. This would tend to corroborate our figure, since attendance from Minneapolis and its suburbs was higher than that from the rest of the Group I area.

But how big actually is the total number of Maybes in the population? How large is the group which is "uncertain" as opposed to "committed" or "turned off?" We must assume that it is larger than the 5 percent of the population which the theatre had attracted; that we had simply failed to communicate well with the rest. Two sets of figures helped us to estimate the total number of Maybes. The same *Star* Metro-Poll found that one of five (20 percent) of those interviewed had seen a stage play during the past year. This included road companies, community theatres, and, presumably, high-school class plays. This, we theorized, could be taken as the outside limit of the Yeses and Maybes combined, since going to see Cousin Julia perform in *Seven Keys to Baldpate* at West Bluff Senior High School is not necessarily indicative of serious theatre-going. For corroborating evidence we looked to the readership figures of the Minneapolis *Sunday Tribune*. What percentage of the population was interested enough in theatre to *read* articles about it in the newspaper?

Of six major stories on theatre events in two different issues of the newspaper (1963 and 1965), the "Read Any" figures ranged from a low of 5 percent on a United Press International feature by Jack Gaver about a new Broadway comedy, to a high of 19 percent on a story about the extension of Theater St. Paul's production of *Three-Penny Opera* given at the Guthrie Theatre.

The figures seemed to corroborate each other. We concluded that a maximum of one-fifth of the population had any interest whatsoever in live theatre. These were the Maybes plus the Yeses. Theoretically, the four-fifths of the population are Noes. But assuming that about 30 percent are either too young, too old, or economically unable to be considered as prospects, our theoretical breakdown came out like this:

Yeses	3 percent
Maybes	17 percent
Noes	50 percent
Ineligible	30 percent

The next job was to determine the type of people who make up each of these groups. And here the waters tend to muddy.

Initially it was assumed that the Yeses, Maybes, and Noes could be separated accurately on the basis of socioeconomic and educational–occupational characteristics. The happy theory was that if the Maybes, who constitute the best immediate potential for audience development, could accurately be identified demographically, they could be reached effectively by selective promotional efforts. The Morison Report suggested that the Yeses were "people of higher educational levels particularly in the liberal arts field, plus those whose earning power or family background had placed them in the higher strata of society." The Maybes, it said, are "people generally on a white collar level including businessmen and professional specialists (engineers, doctors, etc.) whose education has not necessarily brought them into close proximity with the arts." And the Noes, it concluded, were "people quite often on the blue collar level whose comparatively limited education has not allowed them to be introduced to the arts."

It turns out to be more complex. The Yeses, Maybes, and Noes cannot be defined very accurately by demographic characteristics. The only thing that can be stated unequivocally is that a person with a college education earning a relatively high income in the professional or business world *is more likely* to be a Yes or a Maybe than a No. But these characteristics do not prevent a person from having a totally negative attitude toward the arts. From both statistics and the personal experience of the staff, we know that there are large numbers of college-educated, professional men and businessmen earning substantial incomes who simply will not even sample theatre and the arts. We have encountered many who have said quite frankly that they *know* theatre is not their cup of tea. Engineers are educated and earning reasonable incomes. Yet audience-analysis reports from a number of theatres indicate that engineers typically are not interested in theatre. They are Noes. However, they are not automatically and always Noes. There are enthusiastic, theatre-going engineers among the Yeses. We have come to believe that something far beyond just economic-educational-occupational characteristics affects a person's attitude toward theatre and the arts—psychological factors as yet undefined—and there seems to be no existing research on the subject to help to clarify the problem.

There is one bright note of hope. Under a grant from the Rockefeller Foundation, Jack Conrad of Southwestern University is conducting a three-year, in-depth research project to analyze the nature and attitudes of the current audiences at the Front Street Theatre in Memphis, Tennessee. He will compare his findings with information on similar groups who do not attend. We eagerly await his findings which are expected in late 1969 or early 1970. In the meantime, we had to operate on certain speculative conclusions. The matter of the Maybes and our conclusions and questions will be considered in the next chapters. Here, let us present our premise and questions about the half of the population who are Noes.

Perhaps the strongest characteristic which the Noes share is a deep-rooted psychological barrier against the arts—a kind of cultural curtain fabricated independently of socioeconomic or educational–occupational characteristics. This curtain shuts out any association with cultural activities, making people blind and deaf to normal forms of communication about artistic activity, as indicated by the newspaper-readership figures.

Is there validity to this cultural curtain premise? If so, what are the roots of the psychological barrier? Is it possible that they lie almost entirely in the background of class prejudices and fears stemming from this country's seeming tradition of "art for the wealthy few?" Is it necessary or desirable to penetrate this cultural curtain? Can it be done without more extensive knowledge concerning the reasons for its existence? Could this be the time for cultural institutions to conduct a national motivational study regarding attitudes toward the arts?

Chapter 10

A Three-Point Strategy

Rex Partington sat in his backstage office, listmaking —a compulsive preoccupation of production stage managers. A September performance of the 1965 revival of The Miser *was just underway, and the opening lines of dialogue crackled over the loudspeaker. Suddenly Partington cocked an ear and frowned. A line usually good for a rolling laugh had just died. He went back to listmaking but listened intently for the next laugh. It didn't come either.*

An actor on his way to an entrance stuck his head in the office and asked "What's the matter, don't we have anyone out there tonight?" Partington assured him the house was full, but he sat back and listened carefully. A few nervous guffaws began to come, then a light, sweeping titter, and finally a great, full-throated downpour of laughter drenched the house.

Partington smiled and reached for the phone. He recognized now the symptoms of an audience which had never been to the new Guthrie Theatre before— the first hesitancy to react, then the nervous beginnings, and finally, complete relaxation and enjoyment.

"House manager!" Archie Sarazin's voice rattled at the other end of the line. Was there anything un-

usual about tonight's audience, Partington wanted to know.

"I'll say there is," Sarazin replied. "They all came in on books of Gift House Stamps."

The National Food Stores' Gift House Stamp promotion had brought a house full of Maybes into the theatre for the first time, offering further evidence of the validity of the Morison Report's three-point strategy for attracting them. After defining the Yeses, Maybes, and Noes, the report had isolated the Maybes as "the type of person most susceptible to promotion and publicity. This is where the potential lies that must be cultivated and sold."

About the Yeses, the report had said: "We will get them as regular customers. They will come. We cannot ignore them, but we must not overdo the emphasis and effort we place against them." The Noes were virtually dismissed: "We cannot afford to waste time and money on them at this stage. They are a harder sale. They may be long-range prospects, but it is too difficult to sell them in the immediate future."

All three opinions were destined to change by varying degrees in the course of four years.

The Maybes were the prime target. The major problem was defined this way: "How to convince the Maybes that the Guthrie Theatre is *not* so highbrow, cultural, classic, intellectual and socially oriented that they cannot enjoy it, *without* destroying the highbrow, cultural, classic, intellectual and social appeal that is necessary to keep the Yeses in the fold." The problem, it turns out, is universal with American artistic institutions. It is still a problem for the Minnesota Theatre Company.

The report then leapt to a three-point general strategy for selling the theatre to the Maybes and the Yeses:

1. Communicate an image of the Guthrie Theatre as one which puts entertainment and excitement into great drama.
2. The satisfied audiences and admirers of this theatre constitute our best advertising. Use personal recommendation as a primary selling tool.

3. This theatre is not so important to our customers that we can spare any effort to make buying tickets and attending the theater as easy and pleasant as humanly possible.

With characteristic pomposity, the report elaborated. Regarding the matter of image, it said: "We will theme all promotion and advertising around the concept that Guthrie, his company and theatre together are uniquely capable of bringing out the inherent excitement and entertainment in classic theatre without detracting from its philosophic content and pure classicism. Our theme idea will be a frank paraphrase of the New York *Herald Tribune* line, "Great Drama Doesn't *Have* to be Dull!" (If Oliver Rea's better judgment had not prevented that theme line from seeing the light of print, the theatre might conceivably have suffered the same fate as the *Herald Tribune!*)

With respect to point two of the strategy, the report acknowledged the exceptional power of word-of-mouth in theatre, and then continued:

We will recognize and take advantage of this by:

Creating a hard core of devoted personal salesmen for the Guthrie Theatre *within* the primary potential areas in the form of women's organizations, advisory groups, etc.

Developing and exploiting comment and recommendations from important people from *outside* the immediate area. People are always impressed with the opinions of outside authorities about things that are going on in their own backyard . . . often more impressed than they are with opinions of people they know. This should be the primary goal of national publicity efforts.

Developing and exploiting comment, endorsements and testimonial material from among local people who attend the theatre. This should be one of the prime goals of regional publicity.

Finally, regarding point three, the report noted:

Because the Maybes are not sure of themselves in the area of theatre, because there is so much competition for entertainment dollars, because entertainment decisions are often impulse, and because people are becoming used to extreme convenience in all phases of living, there must be developed a spirit of service on the part of all Guthrie theatre employees which brings them to do *anything* to make purchasing of tickets and attending the theatre both easy and pleasant.

Though our wide-eyed naïveté has been dulled by the facts of theatrical life, our egos bruised by a thousand and one failures, and our enthusiasm frustrated by lack of time, money, and energy, we remain convinced of the basic validity of this three-point strategy for audience development. Experience has modified our emphasis and methods of execution, but there is overwhelming evidence that these are the key points.

Even in the example of National Food Stores' Gift House Stamp promotion one can find solid evidence. Here was a houseful of Maybes coming for the first time. What attracted them when two and one half years of previous effort had not? Could it have been the idea of a food chain offering tickets to a Molière play for a book of stamps had communicated a non-highbrow image which had not previously reached them? Could it have been that their neighborhood grocery store, participating in a promotion involving the Guthrie Theatre, constituted a kind of personal endorsement? Could it have been that picking up tickets at the store when they did their weekend marketing was so easy and convenient that it overcame previous inertia? We think it was all three reasons.

Though we remain convinced that much of the basic direction of the Morison Report was sound, our attempts in trying to follow its recommendations have led us to many changes of opinion. We now believe that it is absolutely vital in any audience-development effort *not* to ignore the Noes as first suggested. Work must go on simultaneously on the problems of the Yeses, Maybes, and Noes. Attempts must be made to upgrade continually both the loyalty and the degree of critical knowledge of the Yeses so that they will stick with the theatre in troubled times and continue to challenge it artistically. Yeses must be created from Maybes, and Maybes from Noes. We are further convinced that, not only is it possible to make some headway in piercing the Cultural Curtain that barricades theatre from the Noes, but that *it is absolutely essential to the health of theatre that it be done*. We now believe also that the single most important tool in audience development was hinted at in point two of the three-point strategy: "Create a hard core of personal salesmen." Our experience tells us that primary emphasis for any artistic institution should be on creating ever-widening circles of enthusiastic, dedicated, and evangelistic friends.

Now let us explore how we attempted to make the Morison Report work and what we learned that led us to the foregoing conclusions.

Part Four

The Matter of Image

We must communicate an image of the Guthrie Theatre as one which puts entertainment and excitement into great drama.

The Morison Report

Chapter 11

White Tie and Tennis Shoes

It was the fall of 1961. A splendidly-dressed crowd of the Twin Cities' most promising financial contributors gathered in an oak-paneled dining room of the austere Minneapolis Club to hear a knight of the British Empire speak of classical theatre. At the appropriate moment, Sir Tyrone Guthrie—immaculate in white tie and tails—unfolded his awesome height and launched with eloquence and twinkling irreverence into the exposition of his plan for a theatre in Minnesota.

The next day, in 400,000 homes from Montana to Wisconsin, families scanning their newspapers superficially absorbed a quick, photographic impression of what the Tyrone Guthrie Theatre was to be about: fancy crowds, British knights, exclusive clubs, white ties and tails, and something called "the classics." What they didn't see and didn't know might well have communicated to them a happier and more accurate image of the man and his theatre. At the bottom of his resplendent length, Sir Tyrone Guthrie was wearing a pair of dingy white sneakers.

Image is a word so carelessly bandied about by everyone from Madison Avenue office boys to distinguished motivational researchers that it has become a cliché. It is, nevertheless, a useful word because it accurately describes the total impression which an individual has of an organization—the synthesis of everything he has read, heard, seen, or personally experienced. For someone who has never attended a specific theatre, that theatre's image may consist of what he has glanced at in the newspaper, the way the outside of the building looks, the people he knows who attend, something he overheard in a restaurant, or the way he was treated at the box office when he once phoned to make an inquiry.

Strangely enough, this total impression, or "image"—accurate or inaccurate, rationally or irrationally created—has more influence upon an individual's actions than any other factor, including the most logical sales argument. Image, then, becomes of overriding importance in the creation and operation of any organization or institution.

Concern for image should not imply the creation and presentation of something false or illusory for public consumption. In any set of circumstances, there are gaps between what people *think* an organization is, what the organization *actually* is, and what it *wants to be*. When those gaps are closed, image is no longer a problem. The organization succeeds or fails in a completely honest way—on the basis of true intent and ideals. The aim of management should be to close the gap between what an organization is and what it wants to be. The aim of public relations should be to make the public's image of an organization coincide with what the organization actually is. What muddies the waters is that too many organizations have not clearly defined what they want to be, nor do they come to understand what they really are. In such cases it is inevitable that the public's image will be confused, and steps to improve it will be difficult.

In the days when funds were being raised for a theatre in Minnesota, the public could have no image of what the theatre was because it did not exist. There was no building, no company, no previous production, no precedent with which people were familiar. Despite the efforts of Oliver Rea to sell a triumvirate, the public's image of what the theatre would be was wrapped up in its image of one man—Sir Tyrone Guthrie. And even that image became a bit confused and inaccurate due to the expediencies of fund-raising.

In reality, Sir Tyrone is a man who *does* wear white ties and old tennis shoes, who describes the religious nature of the theatre with salty comments, and who produces his admired classics with an entertaining flamboyance which often evokes screams of anguish from the bastions of intellect and criticism.

The man and the theatre he conceived were a delightful combination of white tie and tennis shoes. But the public synthesized another image—Culture with a very elaborate capital C—despite the fact that Dr. Guthrie continually insisted that theatre should not be considered wholly an educational or uplifting experience but also rousing good entertainment. The public was paying more attention to superficial visual impressions than to the words being spoken.

The image absorbed was largely due to the fact that it is easier to raise large sums of money on the basis of white ties, the religious nature of theatre, and classical plays than of old tennis shoes, salty words, and flamboyance. So the publicity was aimed in that direction. The Yeses in the community came galloping to the aid of the theatre with enthusiasm, money, and eventual ticket-buying support. But since they were vastly outnumbered by the Maybes and Noes, it was evident that from the point of view of long-range ticket-buying, the theatre's image was undesirably overweighted in the wrong direction and was also inaccurate. The Morison Report had correctly defined the problem: How to communicate an accurate image of what Sir Tyrone wanted the theatre to be to those who were a bit afraid of Culture—without alienating those who loved it.

Perhaps if the theatre had remained the idea of one man that problem would have been easier to solve. But soon there was a company, a theatre, an audience, and a season. Instead of these tangibles crystallizing the theatre's philosophy and creating a more accurate public image, the image became more blurred and obscure. The problem became more acute and the solution became more difficult, hampered to some extent by an emerging conflict between the dignity and restraint of the artist and the proclivity toward flamboyance of the promoter—a conflict that was not resolved.

In the first season-ticket brochure distributed in early 1963, a paragraph described the new theatre building as "breathtaking." It seemed an appropriate description to a copywriter whose breath had been taken away by a stunning asymmetrical auditorium of multicolored seats. But hardly had the ink dried when Sir Tyrone strode into the press department, brochure in hand. "Dear boy," he said, "we must not call our theatre breathtaking. Let the people call it that."

So the problem now became how to communicate the image of exciting entertainment in a breathtaking theatre without really saying so, and in the face of rapidly widening gaps between what the theatre wanted to be, what it was turning out to be, and what the public thought it was—and wanted it to be.

Chapter 12

The Major Hurdle

The usual week-night serenity of the small-town country club had been shattered. Golfers just off the course and bound for home, and couples who had planned to have a quick dinner and see a movie, were gathered around Douglas Campbell, who was immensely enjoying his unscheduled floor show. Campbell was at his best, telling the saltiest of salty stories in a dozen dialects, roaring his collection of bawdy English ballads at the top of his considerable voice. The growing crowds loved it.

The impromptu, one-man show had evolved naturally, the result of a day Campbell and Morison had spent in the summer of 1963 exploring a small Minnesota town. At lunch they had met two theatre-loving women who had invited them to dinner at the club. The evening had begun peacefully with the foursome having cocktails while the women's husbands completed their golf game. But hardly had the two golfers ordered their beer when Campbell was off and running with the evening's entertainment.

Eventually he exhausted himself and his repertoire. He and Morison walked out into the warm night air. "Do you know why I did that?" Campbell asked.

"Did what?" Morison hedged.

"Started singing and telling those stories," Camp-
bell replied. Morison admitted he suspected the rea-
sons.

"Because," said Campbell, "I knew those two men
had been dilly-dallying out on the golf course, com-
plaining to each other about their wives forcing them
to have dinner with two artsy, intellectual theatre sis-
sies, and I wanted to prove to them that we aren't
like that."

He may not have known it, but Douglas Campbell was involved
that evening in trying to change the public image of theatre as
a whole, and of all the arts together.

During our four years with the Minnesota Theatre Company we were continually trying to narrow the gap between
what that specific theatre was and what the public thought it
was. But at every turn, we kept running into a bigger problem.
The public was prejudging this specific theatre on the basis of
long-held impressions of what *all* theatre and all Culture were
like. Whenever we did anything which tended to corroborate
this preconceived notion, its validity was automatically rein-
forced in the public mind.

In our opinion, the general public tends to think that arts
and culture are high-society, long-haired, intellectual, artsy,
and sissy. This image is a formidable obstacle to enlarging and
broadening an audience. The question of whether and how the
total image of the arts can be changed must be delayed until we
examine whether the public's impression is actually right. How
much actual difference is there between the reality of the arts
and the public impression or image of them?

From our experience, it seems that there is less difference
between actuality and image than most people connected with
the arts care to admit. As they have existed in our country—
and the Midwest is no exception—the arts *have* been high-
society, long-haired, intellectual, artsy, and sissy to a greater
degree than can be acknowledged with comfort. And further,
there is at least a minority of people within the arts and, indeed, patrons of the arts who seem to prefer it that way. They
do not want to diminish the "mystique" of the arts. They do not

want to broaden the base of the audience because it might force changes in their private world.

If any substantial headway is to be made in the development of larger, more representative audiences, we believe the public image will have to be changed. The question: How can it be done? Can it be done without antagonizing present patrons? It is obvious that no one organization in any community has the resources to change the public image about *all* the arts. It will take a concerted effort.

Chapter 13

The Widening Image Gaps

It was Thursday, May 9, 1963. Stu Baird, then business reporter for the Minneapolis Morning Tribune, was waiting for the weekly luncheon meeting of the Minneapolis Board of Realtors to begin. While he waited, he studied the final edition of the morning paper. For the second straight day, it was filled with stories, pictures and reviews of the Tyrone Guthrie Theatre opening.

Yesterday it had been all over the front page; the review of Guthrie's Hamlet, *pictures of elegant ladies in elegant gowns, social notes, and accounts of the gala champagne party after the performance. Today it was the second opening—Douglas Campbell's enthusiastically received production of* The Miser, *all just as elegant.*

The openings were the topic of conversation during the Realtor's luncheon, too. But when dessert arrived and Minneapolis Assessor Julian R. Garzon was introduced, he turned to the subject of the day: The fiscal problems caused by the growing amount of real estate being exempted from taxation. The speech was going along about as Baird had expected when suddenly he pricked up his ears and made a quick note.

> "I am going to recommend," said Garzon, "that the Tyrone Guthrie Theatre pay real estate taxes."
>
> No more was said in the speech, but Garzon talked willingly with Baird after the meeting. "We feel this is a commercial operation . . . a business," he explained. "I just can't help but wonder how many people in Minneapolis are interested in paying for this luxury.
>
> "The art institute is a community thing," Garzon said. "It provides certain services to the community. It's not on a professional basis. Walker Art Center is a free institution for the people of Minneapolis to enjoy, not just for the select few who are willing to pay $5 to get into it. You get into that area and you are beyond the realm of everyone's pocketbook."

If the public image of the theatre created by the fund drive was a problem in public relations, the image which people drew from the first year of operation constituted a major disaster which should have called for a declaration of administrative emergency. In 12 short months the following gaps appeared between what the theatre wanted and professed to be and what it appeared to be to the public:

1. The theatre wanted to become a community institution independent of any one individual. Instead, it found itself living on the legend of Sir Tyrone. The public waited in awe for the great god of classical theatre to chisel the first tablet of stone. The management quaked at the thought of what might happen when he left at the end of his three-year contract.

2. The theatre professed a "no star" policy, saying "the company" was the true star. It opened rehearsals with a barrage of publicity on Hume Cronyn, Jessica Tandy, Rita Gam, George Grizzard, and Zoe Caldwell. The public lapped it up and bought tickets. The management wondered what they would do next year.

3. The theatre had declared vehemently that it was dedicated to a policy which would prove the great classics can be "splendidly exciting entertainment when well performed." It

opened with a well-performed but soporific four-hour *Hamlet*. The public wiggled, applauded dutifully, sighed quietly, and courageously came back for more. The public relations department just sighed.

4. The theatre claimed it would appeal, and knew it eventually must appeal, to the widest possible cross-section of the community. It opened its doors with the gayest flurry of high social activity since John Philip Sousa came to town to dedicate the Foshay Tower in 1929. The Yeses were delighted. The Maybes said, "I told you it wasn't for us." The Noes paid no attention, and Julian Garzon put the theatre on the city real-estate tax roles.

5. The theatre wanted its company and their work on stage to speak for itself. A dazzling, controversial, and (to some) intimidating piece of architecture took the spotlight in center stage. The public pointed to the building with pride. The management began to view the building with alarm.

6. The theatre was a nonprofit, tax-exempt foundation which knew in its heart that a serious, classical theatre never could be self-supporting. At the end of the first year it proudly and loudly announced a profit of $6,933.14. The public decided the Minnesota Theatre Company must be an enormous success. The board of directors breathed a sigh of relief. The management wondered what they would do next year, and Julian Garzon took the state Attorney General's ruling favoring the theatre's tax exemption to the State Board of Tax Appeals.

For the first time in America, a cultural institution had exploded full-blown upon a community without long years of agonizing struggle against dreadful facilities, insufficient funds, and public indifference. As Oliver Rea puts it, "We planted a full-grown oak instead of an acorn." In retrospect, it seems that the theatre may have paid a rather severe price for The Grand Emergence.

Douglas Campbell had stoutly maintained all along that it would have been wiser to assemble a first-rate company in a grubby, back-street warehouse to demonstrate, without distracting frills, what the theatre was really about.

In retrospect it is clear that the whole staff contributed to the widening of the image gaps. With uncontrolled exuberance, we in public relations plowed into the exploitation of anything we could lay our hands on, with little thought for long-range consequences.

Basically, the theatre was a bit confused about what it wanted to be. But it was also being things it didn't want to be and doing things it didn't want to do *in order* to create an institution on such a grand scale. The theatre *needed* the legend of Sir Tyrone, the glamour of Cronyn, Tandy, Gam, Grizzard, and Caldwell; the elegant flurry of high society; the outrage of a four-hour Ruritanian *Hamlet;* the splendor of a breathtaking building and the pleasant jingle-jangle of box-office success to pull off a caper of such magnitude. But in exploiting these aspects we were helping further to widen the gaps between what the theatre wanted and professed to be and what it appeared to be to the public. We were communicating inaccurate images from which the theatre still suffers.

How much did Sir Tyrone's absence in 1966 contribute to lower attendance? How much did reports of a four-hour *Hamlet,* an uncut *Volpone,* and an obscure *The Way of the World* discourage those who might have been willing to give theatre a try? How much has the theatre's high-society image tended to fortify the cultural curtain among the Noes? When the building is no longer a dazzling attraction, will the public begin to understand what the company is all about? When the inevitable day for deficit fund raising arrives, will the public remember the trumpeted profits of 1963 and 1964 and demand a return to self-sufficiency?

As the hectic days of 1963 progressed, the full implication of what the theatre was doing to its image never dawned on us. We were not aware that we were busily promulgating information which created an image contrary to what the theatre wanted to be and needed to be for long-term survival. But by the grand opening, we began to feel that somehow we weren't doing all we should to communicate the messages which the Morison Report called for. We started to be concerned with paying a little more attention to *what* we were saying, rather than simply with *how much* we said. We began to take direct action to narrow the gap between what people thought the theatre was and what it actually was—and between what the theatre actually was and what it wanted to be. We began to try to correct a distorted public image brought on in good faith and enthusiasm.

Let us recount what we tried to do to right the wrong image of the theatre which the public had acquired by opening night.

Chapter 14

Selective Honesty

"No, really. I don't think we want to let you take pictures in our lobby."

Rob Blake, newly arrived assistant public relations director, was on the telephone in the spring of 1966. A young publicity girl from an out-of-town resident professional theatre sat beside his desk, wide-eyed and incredulous.

"That's right, I'm refusing you permission," Blake continued. "Look at it this way: If you were taking fashion shots of gals in shorts, or sweaters and skirts, that might be different. But we've had enough formal gowns to last us 25 years."

Blake listened patiently to the voice on the other end of the line. "No, I'm not being uncooperative," he answered. "I'm just being practical from our point of view. We can't stand any more high fashion."

Despite his seeming stubbornness, Blake ended the conversation amicably and turned back to his conversation with the visitor. "Was that really a newspaper person on the other end of the line?" she wanted to know.

"Yes, it was," said Blake. "The women's editor of the Minneapolis Star."

Actually turning down an opportunity for publicity would have been regarded as sheer lunacy in the Minnesota Theatre Company press department three years earlier. Rob Blake's refusal to allow pictures of formal fashions to be taken in the theatre lobby reflected a changing attitude toward the role of publicity in the affairs of the theatre. No longer did we tend to measure our effectiveness in the area of publicity by the total number of column inches run in the press. No longer were we willing to accept as applicable to the Guthrie Theatre the traditional goal of press agentry as described by Broadway dean Dick Maney: "to get something for nothing." We no longer considered publicity as an end in itself. It was only a means to many far-reaching ends. Nowhere in this book will the reader find a section on a press department or publicity for, in our opinion, they are not subjects to be considered separately. There will be several chapters in which uses of publicity are described, but only as part of total solutions to the broader problems of audience development.

This attitude toward publicity was not always with us. In the beginning, the press department of the Minnesota Theatre Company *was* a traditional press department. In the first season, the department was headed by Mary Jolliffe as Publicity Director. She is an established professional who had served effectively in the same capacity for many years at the Stratford (Ontario) Shakespeare Festival. To her goes credit for organizing the complex machinery of publicity and press work and for teaching her green colleagues the procedures and traditions of theatrical press agentry. In the first year, Mary Jolliffe had on her staff an assistant publicity director (Cindy Maugham), a publicity assistant (Kay Fliehr), and a Ford Foundation intern, Robert Passoli. Bradley G. Morison served as a part-time public relations consultant.

The change in department designations and titles in four years reflects an evolving concept of the responsibilities of this department of theatre. In 1966, it was called the Public Relations Department, headed by Morison, and had three basic divisions: public information, audience development, and community service. As an indication of where our experiences were taking us, we would now be inclined to call the entire department the community service department with three slightly different divisions of work: communications, education, and sales promotion. Publicity would be considered only as a useful tool in all phases of the work.

One of our primary uses of publicity was to narrow the image gaps. Even though 80 percent of the population may not actually read any of the stories about theatre, many people absorb superficial impressions by glancing at the title, picture, and captions of such stories. Superficial impressions can be misleading, and wrong impressions can cause very potent problems. The full realization of the "image" power of publicity began to hit us when we became aware that random and unrestricted publicity was creating a misleading image.

We were led inevitably to a conclusion best expressed by a public relations professional, John Bos, now managing director of Philadelphia's Theatre of the Living Arts. "Press agentry in resident theatres is the exercise of selective honesty." In essence, he meant that theatres cannot afford to be greedy and undisciplined in their search for publicity. They must seek out only the honest presentation of what they are. This does not imply management or control of hard news. It means primarily that, in the search for feature story material, the temptation must be resisted to use "good copy" if its total impression detracts from, or does not contribute to, the narrowing of the image gap. It means a longer search and more digging to find "good copy" which will make a positive contribution to the solution of the image problem.

Our first realization of the need to be selective came when we began to be aware of the strong "high society" image which the public seemed to have. The Guthrie Theatre may, perhaps, have been more "upper crust" than it wanted to be, but it certainly was not as upper crust as most people believed it to be. We began a conscious effort to pull back. We stopped calling the top society columnist with every social tidbit we encountered. Whenever gracefully possible, we avoided photographs of our more socially prominent women volunteers at teas. Instead, we tried to promote the interesting activities of *all* the theatre's volunteers. We also tried to deemphasize fancy formal dress and the resulting publicity, but with little success. In

1966 we finally eliminated the opening-night party completely. We even managed to persuade our cohorts that members of the staff should not dress for openings. (There are those who think we are completely wrong to diminish the glamor given by formal dress and high society. Certainly care should be exercised and delicate balance achieved. But in our opinion, a larger and broader audience can never be cultivated until the impression is changed that theatre is something exclusively for the wealthy and socially prominent.)

We vowed to try to keep off the women's pages of the newspapers as much as possible and to get on the sports pages, neither of which we managed with much success. Our most spectacular accomplishment resulted from the hiring of a popular, well-known professional wrestler to "direct" the wrestling scene in *As You Like It*. The resulting hilarious account, with pictures, was spread eight columns wide across the top of the front page of the Minneapolis *Star*.

But the society image of the theatre was not the only problem which called for "selective honesty." Despite the fact that Sir Tyrone can make good copy at the drop of a sentence, we found ourselves avoiding the exploitation of his intellectual and witty comments in order to put him in proper perspective to the institution he helped to create. Further, even though the return of Hume Cronyn and Jessica Tandy in 1965 was eagerly awaited by public and press, we found ourselves risking the Cronyns' disappointment by playing them down to emphasize stories about the company in general and the other seemingly-lesser members—all to present the theatre's stated goal of the company itself as the star in proper public perspective. Time after time we deliberately gave up space and broadcast time which would tend to distort what the theatre really stood for, or which would compound the misconceptions.

Another real need for selectivity in publicity didn't come home to us, however, until a conference on long-range audience development was held by the Theatre Communications Group, Inc. at Woodstock, New York, in June of 1966. During the three-day meeting, small groups of theatre people, aided by outside experts, probed for reasons why various categories of the public tended to resist attending theatre. The discussants kept coming back to the fact that great masses of people consider theatre as "sissy" and too feminine. The psychologist at the conference confirmed the fact that attending the theatre and participation in the arts generally ranked very high in femininity on the masculinity–femininity scale. People tend to be scared away because of their "feminine" impression of theatre. Did we, he asked, pay any attention to whether our publicity efforts tended to emphasize or deemphasize the feminine aspects of our theatres? The group members admitted that this had never occurred to them and they mentally reviewed recent publicity. At the Guthrie Theatre that summer we had been particularly proud of a spread we had promoted on the gourmet cooking skills of a male actor. Cooking, the psychologist said, ranked very high on the femininity scale. The image of a man who loved to cook strengthened the image of femininity toward theatre which was detrimental to the development of new audience. It would have been better, we concluded, not to have had the publicity at all. A totally new dimension had been added to the consideration of publicity and its effect upon the image gaps, and new questions had come to our minds.

The roots of promotional efforts for all theatres (and for all the performing arts) are completely entangled in the traditions of Broadway press agentry. But Broadway theatres are essentially selling tickets for their own single shows; this is transient, ephemeral theatre. There is no need for continuity. The image of one production has little effect on the success of another, even when presented by the same producer.

For the new kind of theatre which is emerging, however, the aim is the creation and perpetuation of an institution and its philosophy; the happenings of any one day can greatly affect future years. The long-term image which the public accumulates about a repertory theatre becomes of enormous import to its success or failure, and publicity has a potent influence upon that image. If the nature of theatre is changing, and the role of theatrical publicity changing with it, our experience leads us to ask if the traditional concepts of press agentry, and persons trained in these ways, are not outdated and, in fact, harmful.

Chapter 15

The Company You Keep

"Well, it looks like Camilo Pascual will stay in there. Sam Mele's headed back for the dugout with the count three balls and no strikes on Elston Howard, men on first and third with one out and the Twins leading three to two in the top half of the seventh."

It was Ray Scott, the voice of the Minnesota Twins, broadcasting a Yankee game that summer of 1963 over WCCO, the incredibly dominant radio station which bills itself as "Good Neighbor to the Great Northwest" and lives up to the name.

"All right, Camilo's set . . . he delivers . . . Howard swings . . . Zoilo moves to his left, takes it on one hop . . . over to Allen and on to Mincher . . . double play. The Yankees are out in the seventh, the Twins coming to bat."

Scott changed his ingratiating style of delivery only slightly. "Say, I've got a thought for you Twins fans next time you come to the Cities for a ball game," *he said warmly. "Why not make it a double header and see big-league theatre at its best as well as big-league baseball? The Tyrone Guthrie Theatre is open and running this summer and, believe me, they've got some exciting entertainment for you. There are four different plays running in rotation now, so you have a*

> *choice that suits your taste. And you won't be disap-*
> *pointed, take it from me. For information on tickets*
> *and schedule of performances, just drop me a post*
> *card—Ray Scott here at WCCO in Minneapolis.*
>
> *"And now, here comes Jimmy Hall to lead off the*
> *bottom half of the seventh. . . ."*

A salesman for an FM radio station called it the most idiotic radio purchase he had ever heard of. "All the people who go to your theatre listen to *our* station," he said, "not to baseball games."

For the first four seasons, the only major purchase of radio time made by the Minnesota Theatre Company was a series of twenty-second spot announcements in the broadcasts of the Minnesota Twins games. Why? Not necessarily to sell tickets immediately, although the spots could be expected to act as a reminder for Maybes who had thought about attending a performance. The real purpose was to help narrow the Minnesota Theatre Company's image gaps by putting the theatre in the same frame of reference as baseball. We were deliberately associating the theatre (highbrow, cultural) with the beer-and-hotdogs atmosphere of baseball. The folksy approach of the spots was deliberate; the choice of Ray Scott and other well-known, down-to-earth WCCO personalities was deliberate. Not only was the theatre reaching a large regional audience and associating itself with the "national game" but there was the implication that the theatre was part of the community of hot-dogs, WCCO, home runs, and the Minnesota Twins. We were trying to counterbalance the theatre's image of highbrow society.

A theatre's image, we have said, is the total impression a person has of the organization. The way a telephone is answered, the way a passing traveler is treated when he wants to see the theatre building, the way a disturbed customer is placated at the box office—all can have as much effect on image as a quick impression derived from a glance at a newspaper feature. But another extremely important influence on image is the people and other organizations with which a theatre is associated. "You are known by the company you keep" is an appropriate old adage when it comes to image. As important as any other factor in our efforts to narrow the theatre's image gap was associating it with the kinds of things which would best indicate what kind of an organization the theatre was trying to be.

The association with the Minnesota Twins was not as far-fetched as it might seem. During the first four seasons, a real friendship had developed between the Twins players and the acting company. It became tradition for the company, with the aid of Evy Nordley, company services director, to invite the Twins to a performance and party each season and for the Twins to reciprocate. We avoided too much public exploitation of what was a genuine and pleasant social relationship, but the most successful mat we ever distributed to Midwest dailies and weeklies was a picture of slugger Harmon Killebrew and relief-pitcher Johnny Klippstein being shown around backstage by actor John Cromwell, himself once a semipro ball player.

How successful the baseball spots and other image-correcting efforts were in changing the image is hard to meas-ure. If we had followed through with the pilot town research plan recommended in the Morison Report, we would have had a benchmark of attitudes toward the theatre which would have allowed us to measure any changes. Our personal contacts with the community led us to believe that the baseball association had done considerable good for the theatre's image and had also cut a hole in the Cultural Curtain to chip away at the fear-of-culture wall. The association with WCCO radio personalities who delivered the baseball spots was almost as important to this concept as the association with baseball itself. The WCCO staff are well-known, highly-respected members of the commu-nity whose personalities and style appeal to a broad cross-section of the people in the area. We looked for further ways to associate the theatre with WCCO.

Early in the 1963 season it became evident that the thea-tre's Wednesday matinee was the weakest performance, pri-marily because the Twin Cities did not have the matinee habit. We began to investigate the possibilities of special matinee luncheons, and then the welcome thought hit us that the the-atre might cosponsor such luncheons with WCCO. The promotion staff of the station, in its tradition of support for civic enterprises, was eager to cooperate. WCCO personalities would promote the luncheons on the air and also appear as masters of ceremony and hosts for the affairs. The WCCO–Guthrie Matinee Parties were planned in cooperation with a third sponsor, Minneapolis' newest and most glamorous hotel, the Sheraton-Ritz. By happy circumstances we could combine the folksiness of WCCO's good-neighbor approach with the lure of lunching at the newest, swankiest hotel in the city.

Each week for twelve weeks the pattern was the same. WCCO, on hundreds of radio and TV spots, would promote the luncheon, the play, the members of the company who would be present, and the radio or TV personality who would act as host. Charles Carey, manager of the Sheraton-Ritz, would call forth the best efforts of his staff to make the ladies feel welcome and important. After the luncheon, the WCCO personalities would interview two or three members of the acting company and everybody would happily board chartered buses for the theatre, wearing specially-printed name tags announcing the "WCCO-Guthrie-Sheraton-Ritz Matinee Party." The total package price: six dollars and ninety-five cents, including parking at the hotel garage.

Even with excellent cooperation among the sponsors there were costs involved. The theatre provided art work; WCCO printed the materials in its print shop. The hotel cut its luncheon cost to the bone and advertised the matinee parties in its regular schedule of mailings and promotion. All other costs were split three ways.

But the results were rewarding. Suddenly, going to a Wednesday matinee at the Tyrone Guthrie Theatre became an occasion, and the matinee parties came close to running at the full capacity of the Sheraton-Ritz Ballroom—about 300 persons. The theatre increased attendance for Wednesday matinees and reached women who might not otherwise have attended the theatre without the convenience and excitement of the parties. An extra benefit was increased public awareness that the theatre gave Wednesday afternoon performances. But, for all three sponsors, the main and valuable benefit came from this association with each other.

In 1964, because of rumblings from other business sources, it was decided to spread the luncheons around to different hotels in St. Paul as well as in Minneapolis, keeping the formats of the programs the same. The weakness in St. Paul, pinpointed by the audience-analysis research in 1963, led us to include that city. Twelve such parties were held but response was varied, with the audiences ranging from a low of 24 one bleak Wednesday in St. Paul to a high of 340 when George Grizzard was the speaker at a Minneapolis meeting. The reasons for this fluctuation are unclear. Whether women were confused by the constantly changing locations, or whether they had already decided on matinee idols and would not turn out for anyone else are matters for conjecture. But after the second series in 1964, the matinee parties were dropped. We now think the parties were dropped too soon, but they had served their primary purpose beautifully.

Whenever possible, we used similar associations to help convince the Maybes and the Noes that the Guthrie Theatre wanted to be part of the whole community, not just to provide highbrow entertainment for the few. The Theatre's cooperation in the National Food Stores' Gift House Stamp promotion, for example, was another such association. An AFL-CIO night promoted during the first three seasons was also aimed more at closing the image gap by association than simply at "selling a house." Those who came to these affairs were pleasantly surprised at what they found, and many became good salesmen for the theatre within the union ranks. But the unions had difficulty selling 1,437 seats and the union night was dropped in 1966. We had not yet had sufficient time to improve the theatre's image and to change enough Noes to Maybes.

Another chance to improve the image through association literally fell in our laps when the Minneapolis Chamber of Commerce announced to us early in 1964 that it wanted to have a civic luncheon honoring the entire Minnesota Theatre Company. The Chamber of Commerce had made similar luncheons for the Twins baseball and Vikings football teams a tradition. Now the Chamber members wanted to tell the city that they were proud of the theatre and what it had come to mean to the community. Consequently, at the beginning of the second season, some 700 persons gathered at the Leamington Hotel—having paid for the privilege of sloshing through a spring downpour—to honor 65 members of the company. George Grizzard, ill with a cold and laryngitis, felt the occasion so important that he got out of bed against orders and proudly took his place at the long head table. The Guthrie trumpets opened the festivities, the Governor and the Mayor spoke, and suitable plaques were presented to Oliver Rea and Tyrone Guthrie. It marked the first time a theatre organization had been so honored by a civic group.

While we were working through publicity on the problems of the "dress-up" image given by press coverage of opening nights, we were also trying to work at the problem through association and example.

One attempt to change this image was through the film "Miracle in Minnesota," which tells the story of the Guthrie Theatre. In one sequence a station wagon is shown driving up to the theatre sporting a Kansas license plate and with a canoe roped to its top. (Though re-created in the film, the incident actually happened in the summer of 1963). Alighting from the car are two women in simple cotton dresses and a man in a sport shirt. Again, further on in the film when the audience close-ups are shown, there is an older man with an open-necked sport short attentively watching a performance of *Hamlet*.

Evidently we were too subtle, for speakers showing the film knew an inevitable question from the women would be: "What is appropriate dress for the theatre?" This query was particularly predominant in the smaller towns.

Perhaps a more successful attempt to reduce the formal-dress image, which had been created by press coverage of opening nights, was through the use of association. At each opening night the theatre invited a section of the press for a special event. *The Cherry Orchard* was scheduled to open in July of 1965, a time when we had been giving particular thought to the problems of the "dress-up" image. Since the women's editor of the local paper and the women's director of the local radio or

TV station are two of the best channels for reaching women in small towns, the theatre invited all the women's editors and broadcast directors within the one-hundred-mile area, plus many from larger cities in the five-state region. The invitations read: "Buffet supper and style show—fashions for the Guthrie."

On opening night one hundred and sixty-two women editors and directors arrived at the Capp Towers Motor Hotel (now the Holiday Inn) fully expecting to see fashions from the exclusive Oval Room at Dayton's department store. Instead they saw fashions presented by Sears Roebuck! All were in excellent taste, yet available to anyone no matter what the size of one's town or pocketbook.

The member of the promotion staff at Sears Roebuck, themselves eager to establish their store's image as a place where people could buy clothes for any occasion, were delighted to cooperate. We did run into one problem: We asked that one of the male models wear an open-necked sport shirt, but the stylist for Sears rebelled. It would "disturb" their image she said, and we were forced to compromise with a buttoned-neck sport shirt and no tie!

The dinner and the Sears Roebuck style show were reported by dozens of newspapers and broadcast stations in the Midwest and, hopefully, some additional headway was made toward narrowing the image gap by association. Association used as a method to correct image; publicity used as a tool to communicate the message.

We were remiss in not pursuing further cooperative efforts with Sears Roebuck. They were willing to explore the possibility of window displays in all their regional stores, tying in their fashions as appropriate wear for the Guthrie Theatre and prominently displaying the theatre's posters and production photos. Such displays, emphasizing the association with Sears, would have been invaluable in correcting the theatre's image. Again, lack of time prevented us from following an excellent opportunity.

There were many other opportunities during four years to narrow the theatre's image gaps through association which are not related here, and also many which we overlooked or had no time to follow. But, using the twin tools of association and selectivity in publicity, we had made a start.

There was another important factor affecting image that also had to be attended to: The printed image. Here we met with somewhat less success.

Chapter 16

Color, Words, and Design

Dear boy, we must not say our theatre is breathtaking.
Let the people say it.   TYRONE GUTHRIE
What we need is more pizzazz in our printed stuff and
promotion. More show biz.   OLIVER REA
I absolutely despised those purple and green colors we
used on last year's brochure.   TANYA MOISEIWITSCH
Now we're getting somewhere. The orange and ma-
genta in the Op art design are more memorable—like
the purple and green in 1964.   OLIVER REA
Take out that "autumn adventure in theatre." I just
don't want it used.   PETER ZEISLER
I guess we have to tell people what the plays are about,
but why do we have to use so many adjectives?
                          DOUGLAS CAMPBELL
I'd like to have a brochure with a plain white cover
and small type in the lower right-hand corner that said
"Minnesota Theatre Company—1965 season."
                          OLIVER REA

*Your 1965 brochure is terrible. It looks like the annual
report for a bank. Or a funeral parlor.*

DANNY NEWMAN

Dear girl, we don't have to tell *people what the plays
are about. Just tell them the names and the fact that
we're* doing them. TYRONE GUTHRIE

The trouble with the theatre is that everybody *there is
an artist.* BOB ENGLUND. *BBD&O art director*

When it came to the matter of its printed image, the Minnesota
Theatre Company was the victim of multiple schizophrenia.

The Morison Report had called for the communication of
an image of the Guthrie Theatre as one which "puts entertainment and excitement into great drama." "This theatre," it said,
"is uniquely capable of bringing out the inherent excitement
and entertainment of classic theatre without detracting from
its philosophic content and pure classicism."

We were charged with projecting through words and
graphics an image of exciting contemporary classicism. Or was
it to be exciting classic contemporaneity? Or perhaps contemporary classic excitement? Or classical contemporary excitement?

The confusion stemmed basically from the fact that what
the theatre was and what it wanted to be were still neither
clearcut nor agreed upon. The theatre was, and still is, in the
process of evolution. The problem was compounded by the fact
that when there was agreement on what the theatre was, there
was disagreement among people obviously talented in the visual and verbal arts of theatre over how best to *communicate*
what was agreed upon. There was the age-old conflict between
the artist and the promoter—the conflict between dignified restraint and exuberant flamboyance. (It is something of an
enigma that Dr. Guthrie, who can be flamboyant on stage,
would plump for such conservative restraint in promotion.)

The whole schizophrenic dilemma would be laughable if
it were not so important. Graphics and words have a great

effect upon the image which the public receives about an organization. A theatre must rely heavily on display and printed material and can suffer untold damage to its image—and its profits—by an unwise choice of words and/or graphics.

In the market place, packaging has tremendous influence in attracting first-time buyers. For a theatre, its printed material is part of its packaging. Even outside the realm of packaged goods, style and consistency of graphic image have an increasing effect upon the image and eventual success of large corporations and other institutions. Trademarks, letterheads, advertising styling, and communication language, rightly or wrongly, are often crucial in success or failure. There seemed to be no lack of appreciation of these precepts within the Minnesota Theatre Company, only disagreement over what the theatre stood for and how to communicate it.

The first graphic symbol used by the theatre was the "Flying G" designed by Rob Roy Kelley of the Minneapolis School of Art. There was substantial agreement that this was an excellent trademark, one which was both attractive and easily identifiable.

Unfortunately, it stood for the wrong thing. The G signified the building and the man, rather than the company. This was the Minnesota Theatre Company playing in the Tyrone Guthrie Theatre, a distinction which the public still has difficulty in making. But it was an important distinction to communicate, for the intent was that the company would play in many places throughout the Midwest. In 1967, it is the Minnesota Theatre Company playing at the Tyrone Guthrie Theatre in Minneapolis and the Crawford Livingston Theatre in St. Paul.

The graphics for the first season were based upon this "Flying G." The poster carried it strongly. It was exhibited boldly on the brochure and served as the cover design of the souvenir program.

But as the 1964 season approached, it was decided to begin playing down the "Flying G" and to develop a different graphic approach for every season. The decision to refrain from developing a *single* substitute symbol for all future seasons was based on two premises:

1. What the company wanted to be, what it was, and what it would eventually become was still in a state of flux. It would be difficult for some years to develop a truly reflective graphic symbol which could be expected to be lastingly appropriate.
2. It seemed important, at least in the first few years, to do everything possible to generate new excitement for every new season. Startling changes in graphics each year would help to project the idea that something new was about to happen.

In the second season we developed as a graphic symbol a representative coat of arms with separate symbols for each of the four plays. It was reasonably effective (though criticized by some internal sources as being too formal and stuffy) and was deceptively easy to do. The plays happened to lend themselves to easy visualization: *Henry V*, a crown; *Saint Joan*, Joan's sword; *Volpone*, a fox; *The Glass Menagerie*, a unicorn with broken horn. But following seasons were not as easy.

Theatres promoting one production at a time can create graphics symbolizing that one play. Trying to create one symbol for a series of plays was a different matter. In the third season, we used an architectural interpretation of the stage itself, done in shades of brown and orange. The orange and brown design of the stage, however, proved bland compared with the color scheme of the previous season. In 1964 there had been no question in the public's mind that anything purple and green had something to do with the Guthrie Theatre. In 1965, while the graphics were pleasant, they were not memorable.

In 1966, we strove for something more startling—Rea's "pizzazz." The theme of the year was the Twin Bill—a two-part season. We chose two checkerboard semicircles of black, orange, and magenta—done *à la* Op art—to communicate the twin idea. The design worked from the viewpoint of readily identifying anything magenta and orange as belonging to the Guthrie Theatre for 1966. (Some people also associated the theatre with anything that made them dizzy.)

But a yearly change of graphics was difficult. It was very demanding to ask that a superb, artistic, and readily identifiable combination of colors and graphic symbols be created every season.

By the end of 1966 we thought we had arrived at a solution which would satisfy the graphic needs of the theatre and add immeasurably to the artistic integration of the community. Our plan was to commission each year a local painter to do a nonrepresentative painting capturing the philosophy and spirit of the season. The painting would be hung in the lobby, and from it would be extracted the colors and design elements for all printed material. The painting itself—in four-color photographic reproduction—would grace the brochure, the souvenir program, and other printed materials. The scheme seemed ideal. There would be continuity from year to year in the concept of paintings, yet a fresh sense of excitement brought by each new artist. The image projected would be one of contemporary style in the classic medium of painting. And there would be many possibilities for publicity and merchandising. Unfortunately, we left the theatre before we had the opportunity to give the plan a trial.

The question of whether it is better for a theatre to have strong graphics which carry over from one season to the next or to use a fresh approach for each new year remains unanswered in our minds. There are strong arguments for each approach. One style, used indefinitely, would seem to create a stronger image for the public and, over the long run, would project a more definite viewpoint. On the other hand, a theatre is literally manufacturing and marketing a new product with every play, and static graphics cannot capture and project the sense of excitement and newness which is part of the theatrical milieu.

The answer may lie in a compromise—a combination of a strong continuing trademark style coupled with fresh, symbolic designs for each new season or play. Every theatre or artistic institution should have some well-designed logotype or trademark, along with identifying colors and typographic style, to give continuity to letterhead, signs, calling cards, and other pieces. The "Flying G" served this purpose for the Minnesota

Theatre Company. Even though it was the wrong symbol, it was kept constantly in sight (although relegated to secondary prominence) on all promotional material.

The subject of the effect of graphics on what the public thinks of the organization is fascinating and complex. Finding a style or combination of styles which will correctly communicate what an institution stands for is extremely difficult. We were far from successful in our attempts, and we strongly suspect that, in some cases, our efforts in audience development may have been hampered more than helped by the nature of our printed image. In all our work in the area of promotional material—from graphic design to copywriting and printing—we found continual conflict between artistic and promotional viewpoints. Each side's arguments are often equally valid. There are times when the exuberance of a promoter needs toning down. But there does seem to be an inherent conflict, basically due to a lack of understanding of each other's problems.

The strict time schedules necessary for a successful promotion campaign are seemingly incomprehensible to the artistic staff which can change almost at will up to opening-night curtain. No promotion man can consider himself a professional until he has tried to explain to a director that the request to "change those two names around and add this one" can mean damaging expense in plate change, press waiting time, additional art and type charges, and disastrous delays in promotion schedules. In four years we never truly found an adequate formula for compromise between the artistic and promotional viewpoints. We tried to anticipate changes and to allow time and budgetary leeway; we got initialed approval on all layouts and copy to forestall later arbitrary changes; we wheedled and cajoled; we reasoned and talked cost; we stormed and ranted. And, in the end, frustrated, tired and defeated, we made the changes. In a last-ditch attempt to maintain our equilibrium, we adopted the conclusion that it was just part of the game—just "show biz."

The problem is one of communication as well as of philosophy. If the conflict between artistic and promotional viewpoints can ever be resolved, the answer must be education—

both ways. Each must learn more about the other's problems and make a concerted effort to understand the other's viewpoint. In the sack race to build any artistic institution the artistic and promotional staffs who can coordinate their steps will win the prize—permanence.

Part Five

Ever-Widening Circles

The satisfied audiences and envious admirers of this theatre constitute our best advertising. . . . We must create a hard core of devoted personal salesmen within the prime potential area in the form of women's organizations, advisory groups, etc.

The Morison Report

Chapter 17

The Whites of Their Eyes

It was an unseasonably warm day in early May of 1963 when a distinguished, energetic man in a gray suit hailed a cab outside the Twin Cities Metropolitan Airport and asked to be taken to a downtown Minneapolis hotel. As the taxi swung onto the freeway and picked up speed, the cabbie glanced back at his passenger. "Ever been here before, Mister?" he asked.

The traveler indicated that this was his first time in Minneapolis. "Great place," said the cabbie. "Lotsa things going on. Y'know what you oughta do if you got time? You oughta take in this new Gunthrie Theatre we got." The visitor expressed interest. "Funny lookin' place," the cabbie observed. "But the shows are great. This Hugh Crow guy, man, can he act. He really kills you in this show about a miser. You oughta see it."

As it turned out, the newcomer didn't need the cabbie's urging, for the Tyrone Guthrie Theatre was his ultimate destination. But the enthusiasm of the taxi driver was impressive enough so that a report of it eventually showed up in The New York Times. *The passenger was Howard Taubman.*

It is hardly revolutionary in theatrical circles to suggest that "word of mouth" is a potent force in success or failure. So it is not particularly astounding that the Morison Report stated that this constituted "our best advertising" and recommended the creation of a hard core of personal salesmen and the exploitation of favorable comment from outside and inside the primary market area. It remained for a series of happy accidents which occurred over the first two years to demonstrate the true power of personal recommendation and to help crystallize a philosophy which could help unleash that power.

There are those in the ivory towers of art—and indeed within the walls of the Guthrie Theatre—who believe that "word of mouth" needs no stimulation and that all marketing and selling activities are unnecessary and somehow degrading. Simply present a brilliant production, they say, and the audiences will come. This is not true. Decades ago the business world recognized and accepted the premise that the world will no longer beat a path to your door because you build a better mousetrap. It doesn't happen here, and it doesn't happen now. There are too many people, too many new kinds of mice, too many better mousetraps, and too many people telling about them by too many means of communication.

These are the facts: No business, industry or institution can stay in business while waiting for natural person-to-person communication to spread the word about a good product. There is neither time nor money to wait that long.

It is necessary today to *speed up* the process of communication about a product, service, or idea—to make something which will eventually happen occur fast enough for the organization to survive the interim. This is the basic function of marketing, advertising, and promotion—and of audience-development efforts for a theatre.

Most of the audience-development efforts for the Minnesota Theatre Company were concerned with finding ways to accelerate word-of-mouth communication. The promoting cabbie was a happy accident which gave us some clues. A few days before the opening of *The Miser,* director Douglas Campbell exploded into the theatre's administrative offices. He announced that he must have a full house for a preview performance the next evening. The half-dozen assorted people who then comprised the press department flew to their telephones and called anyone they knew who could deliver a substantial quantity of warm bodies. To some unidentified genius among them should go a medal for calling the taxi companies and inviting their drivers. In short order, Minneapolis became the only city in America with a corps of cabbies who overwhelmed their passengers with conversations about Molière.

The effectiveness of the taxi driver's enthusiasm was only one of the clues that began to show us the enormous powers of person-to-person communication. Danny Newman, the Theatre Communications Group's consultant on season-ticket selling, had met with The Stagehands on a Sunday morning in late 1962. He convinced them of the value of coffee parties, and by the opening of the season-ticket drive in January, 1963, there were enough neighborhood gatherings scheduled to warm the heart of any political campaign manager.

The question then was what to do when the gatherings gathered. The theatre was still an intangible. There were no exciting pictures of last year's productions, no rave reviews from past seasons, no movies or slides—nothing concrete to present. The only solution was to have members of the theatre staff who, hopefully, had some idea of what would eventually happen on stage try to describe coming events in person. To Barton Emmet, administrative director, Ford interns Bill Boughton and Bob Passoli, and Oliver Rea went the assignment of fighting winter blizzards, consuming tens of thousands of three-layer, pimento-cheese sandwiches, and dredging up millions of descriptive words about what the coffee drinkers would see on stage at the Guthrie Theatre. At the same time, hundreds of clubs and organizations were stimulated in their curiosity by the barrage of publicity that was being released. Program chairmen, always desperate to fill the year's schedule, began to ask the theatre for speakers. So the intrepid band of representatives from the theatre, clutching boxes of throat lozenges, hit the creamed-chicken circuit. When their seemingly endless energy flagged, they were aided by hastily recruited and trained volunteers flung into the breach. Emmet himself set what must be a record by giving one hundred and ten major speeches between late January and the end of May 1963.

When the dust settled, the Minnesota Theatre Company

had sold more season tickets than had ever been sold up to that time by any American theatre. (Details of the drive are outlined in a subsequent chapter.) The primary reason for the success became evident: Personal contact!

What should have been readily apparent to trained advertising-promotion people began to dawn on us: The best kind of selling is the communication of *personal enthusiasm* for a product, service, or idea. There is no better audience-development technique than person-to-person contact. Publicity, advertising, and direct mail are, at best, merely substitutes. From then on, a high percentage of the Public Relations Department's energy went into finding ways to stimulate personal contact between the theatre's staff and company, its devotees and the public.

Through the experiences outlined in this section, point two of the Morison Report strategy evolved into an unshakable belief: The most fruitful method of developing audiences is the creation of ever-widening circles of dedicated evangelists.

Chapter 18

Volunteers

A letter received January 23, 1965, from a member of the board of the Duluth (Minn.) chapter of The Stagehands:

Dear Kay:

Here is the bill for expenses for the past two months that you asked me to send you.

Bus to Mpls. for Mrs. Helling	$1.55
Telephone calls to Superior, Wisc.	1.00
Bus to Eveleth and return	.85
Yoho Photography (film repair)	6.00
Tow truck hauling out of drift during film delivery	2.00
	11.40

I showed the film to 3,500 children and 712 adults in the last two months.

Some of these expenses may be above and beyond the call of the Guthrie.

My husband said he was willing to pay for the new fender inasmuch as I had already dented it before I went into the snowdrift, but he balked at paying the tow charges.

We really came out of the experience quite well.

76210

Johnny's toe, which was frost-bitten when he walked
for the tow truck, is back to normal size.

I had planned to come to Minneapolis next week,
but I chipped my front tooth on the steering wheel
when I skidded into the drift and won't be through
with the dentist until week after next. So I'll plan to
see you then.

> *Cordially,*
> *Biz Spencer*

Mrs. Spencer's bill should have been presented directly to the
triumvirate of Guthrie, Rea, and Zeisler. Like the house that
Jack built, their idea for a regional repertory theatre propelled
a steering committee in Minneapolis to action, which inspired
a finance committee into a fund campaign, which involved
thousands in giving money, which led to 1,400 women selling
season tickets, which brought about the creation of The Stagehand's women's volunteer organization, which led to the recruitment of The Stagehands in towns outside the metropolitan
area, which led to the formation of a Duluth chapter, which led
to Mrs. Spencer volunteering to schedule the film, *Miracle in
Minnesota,* in icy, snowy, hilly Duluth . . . which eventually
netted a dentist a comfortable fee and gained the Guthrie Theatre a growing audience in a city 157 miles north of Minneapolis.

The Morison Report had recognized the need for volunteers. It had recommended major use of women volunteers for
the season-ticket drive. It suggested a men's volunteer organization to be called The Producers, and recommended a program
of "Town Representatives"—volunteer representatives in major
towns and cities throughout the five-state area who would serve
as a communications link between the theatre and their communities.

It failed to envision the many ways in which volunteers of
all kinds made invaluable contributions to the public relations
and communications goals of the theatre, however. Personal
contact in the community by volunteers is crucial to the development of the ever-widening circles of dedicated evangelists
which we now believe to be so important. The management

which can mobilize and coordinate the public relations potential of its volunteers can increase many times the effectiveness of its audience-development manpower and money. Unfortunately we began to understand the importance of this concept too late in our association with the theatre to fully capitalize on it.

The central volunteer group of the Minnesota Theatre Company was, of course, its board of directors. Like most boards of directors, its overwhelmingly important contribution was acceptance of financial responsibility for the organization. As is also accepted practice, the week-to-week problems of the board were delegated to an executive committee. This left some 70 board members—community leaders of stature from five states—with little to do except to attend quarterly meetings of the full board. Their enthusiasm was not fully utilized. There were those board members who understood their value in public and community relations and, on their own incentive, carried out important projects. One board member gave countless lectures on the theatre each year. Another worked constantly with the schools and libraries in her community promoting the Guthrie Theatre. It was the excellent community relations work of two Duluth board members which paved the way for the establishment of a Stagehands chapter.

But volunteers can be most effective in public relations activity only when their efforts are closely coordinated with the master strategy. Had we carefully planned programs in which board members were involved, they could have been of immeasurable help in creating the best community environment for the theatre. Failure to make better use of the board of directors was our error. We also failed to complete plans for a men's volunteer organization and for the "Town Representatives." The Producers was conceived primarily as a sales force to promote ticket sales to business and industry. Such a volunteer organization probably could have done effective work in this area, but we now see that their greatest value could have been as an extension of the Public Relations Department. The pressure of other seemingly more important projects in the initial season prevented the creation of this group of volunteer men. Lack of time was also responsible for our failure to develop the

Town Representatives program as originally conceived, although The Stagehands and the board members helped to fill the void in many of the outlying towns.

In the four years, however, we did manage to create valuable volunteer advisory committees. Groups of educators, librarians, teenagers, and labor leaders served the theatre well in many areas of public and community relations. (These committees will be dealt with more completely in later chapters.) But it was with the women's organization—The Stagehands—that the theatre made the most effective use of volunteers (the official name of the organization was The Tyrone Guthrie Theatre Stagehands League, Inc., although it was popularly referred to as The Stagehands.)

It would be satisfying to be able to say that The Stagehands were carefully organized and completely planned, but, as Phyliss Wohlrabe, the woman primarily responsible for the organization, has stated: "We just grew like Topsy." Mrs. Wohlrabe, who had volunteered her time and services for two years during the fund-raising drive, was asked by Oliver Rea to gather together other interested volunteers to concentrate on the vital task of selling season tickets for the first season. No one, not even the theatre's artistic or managing directors, knew whether the public would accept the theatre's productions. The women were being asked to sell a pig in a poke—and quite an expensive pig at that, at eighteen dollars for the top-priced season ticket. Only their personal enthusiasm for the theatre's ideals could be marketed.

Undaunted, 35 women who had already given their time to raise funds for the building took on the new assignment. Each one brought an interested friend to an initial meeting where they were wooed and won by Guthrie's persuasive charm into recruiting even more friends to promote season tickets. Eventually, 1,400 women communicated their enthusiasm so well that 21,295 season tickets were sold before opening night of the new theatre. Finally, after completing their first major job, the women were formally organized into The Stagehands. This haphazard method of developing such an important public-relations force is not recommended. (More proper and effective organization is discussed with excellent clarity in

Helen M. Thompson's *Handbook for Symphony Orchestra Women's Associations,* published by the American Symphony Orchestra League.)

In addition to selling season tickets, The Stagehands' initial activities were the important but traditional ones for any women's organization—office and clerical work, maintaining the press clipping book, supplying transportation for actors and visitors, ushering for high-school matinees, knitting chain mail armor for the costume shop, and other sundry jobs. But with the creation of The Stagehands' speakers' bureau and the training of guides to conduct backstage tours, the women began to become more directly involved in public relations. Efforts were made to coordinate The Stagehands' activities more closely with overall public relations strategy.

The Stagehands never had been a "social" organization to the extent that many such women's volunteer organizations are. But, perhaps because its original membership was not truly a representational cross-section of the community, the public seemed to have the impression that it was more a "society" group than it actually was. When we began to recognize the great value of women volunteers in communicating with the whole community, we began to see the necessity of making its membership more representative of the whole community. Efforts were made to recruit members on a geographical basis as well as to be representative of many different groups. A business and professional division of The Stagehands was organized, for instance. The efforts to broaden the base of membership were never as successful as we wished, but some headway was made.

The creation of the Duluth chapter of The Stagehands was an experiment in creating a women's organization solely for the public relations purposes. The group was given total responsibility for the organization of a local speakers' bureau; the booking of the film; personal contact with the community's media, schools, libraries, clubs, and civic organizations; and the handling of publicity in the Duluth area. It operated in close relationship with the Public Relations Department and adhered to the general outlines of the department's philosophy, though free to use its own judgment in coping with local conditions. The experiment was a resounding success and plans were being formulated for the creation of similar chapters in other cities. Encouraged by the enthusiasm with which The Duluth Stagehands had accepted and carried out major public relations responsibilities, we decided to test further our evolving theory that a women's volunteer organization would be most valuable when serving as an extension of the Public Relations Department.

In early 1966, faced with more projects than manpower, we asked The Stagehands' president, Mrs. John Linner, if there were women in the organization with a background of professional experience who would willingly accept responsibility for major projects under the direction of the Public Relations Department. There were. A dozen women with degrees in journalism, education, and theatre were chosen for the first experiment. They were told they would have a large amount of creative responsibility, little help, and less credit. They would be treated as demandingly as if they were members of the public relations staff. This group became the "special projects division" of The Stagehands. In short order, with great skill and competence and no rewards except personal satisfaction, they accomplished the following:

1. *Project Film Strip:* Written, produced and managed by a theatre major and a former school teacher, showing the evolution of a costume from conception to completion.
2. *Project Newsletter:* Planned, written, and edited by two ex-journalists and sent bimonthly to subscribers.
3. *Project Press Conference:* Planned, organized, and executed by two former teachers, involving journalism students and their advisors from all high schools in the Twin Cities and suburban area.
4. *Project Teen Advisory Council:* Organized and directed by two former school teachers. An organization of top students from every high school in the area to give the theatre advice on attracting young people to the theatre.
5. *Project Research:* A depth-interview research project carried out by a team of ten Stagehands working with BBD&O.

The enthusiasm and skill with which members of the Special Projects Division accepted and carried out major responsibility led us to the conclusion that we had barely scratched the surface in utilizing such volunteer talents. We have concluded that the extent of major work that can be planned, totally supervised, and executed by volunteers is endless—*if* the volunteer organization is properly organized, and *if* the institution gives wholehearted cooperation. The increase in scope which such volunteer work could give to public-relations and community-service programs is enormous.

In the light of our experience and the changing relationship of the arts to their communities, we are compelled to ask if the time has come for a long, hard look at the usually accepted concepts of volunteer organizations. Traditionally, a majority of the activities undertaken by women's volunteer organizations have been social in nature. From our experience, the public seems to associate such organizations with high-society artistic dilettantes. This image would seem, in our opinion, to be detrimental to the development of broad community support. A gala social aura may attract and hold a certain number of women, but if a volunteer organization is to be viewed as having meaningful, major responsibilities in areas of community relations, we question whether such a membership is too narrow and too shallow. Can the arts afford the luxury of women's volunteer organizations who are predominantly socially oriented? Would volunteer organizations be more valuable in light of the changing times if members were to be recruited on the basis of needed talent, skills, and experience as well as to be more representative of the whole community? Shouldn't major volunteer organizations include men as well as women? Since half of this country's population is under twenty-five years of age, shouldn't volunteer organizations reflect this in their membership?

Volunteers, organized or individuals, are the important nucleus of the "hard core of dedicated personal salesmen" called for by the Morison Report. They will communicate personal enthusiasm for the theatre with a vengeance because they are personally involved and that involvement makes it their theatre. If the circles of dedicated evangelists for the theatre are to continue to widen, it will depend to a large extent on the continuing recruitment of a broader variety of volunteers and their involvement in important areas of community relations.

Chapter 19

Unaccustomed as I Am . . .

An American Airlines Astrojet bound for Chicago lumbered slowly into the night and out to the end of the runway at New York's Kennedy Airport and stopped. The engines settled into a soft whine while five, then ten, then fifteen minutes passed. Brad Morison, making notes for the speech he was to give the following noon to the AAUW in Cedar Rapids, Iowa, occasionally glanced at his watch, wondering if he would make his connecting flight at O'Hare in Chicago. Eventually the plane headed back for the terminal while the captain explained. A February blizzard was raging across the Midwest and Chicago's airport had been closed down.

Back in the terminal, Morison put in a midnight call to Kay Fliehr in Minneapolis. Could she get someone to fill his speaking date in Cedar Rapids the next day? Driving was almost impossible, Kay reported, but she'd try.

While the snow flew outside their meeting place the following day, the ladies of the Cedar Rapids AAUW listened intently as a peppery, eloquent man with a Master's degree in theatre from Northwestern University spoke on the assigned topic: The place of theatre in our lives today. He was Don Tescher, director of the Cedar Rapids Community Playhouse.

With the realization of the importance of personal contact, the Public Relations Department of the Minnesota Theatre Company made a decision: No one anywhere in the five states who was interested in theatre would ever be turned down in a request for a speaker. Obviously, this kind of commitment called for a corps of speakers much larger than the heroic platoon who fought the Coffee Party Campaign of 1963. It called for the cooperation of the entire staff and company, and eventually the help of hundreds of volunteer friends (such as Don Tescher) beyond the walls of the Tyrone Guthrie Theatre.

During 1963 staff members who were veterans of the ticket campaign, aided by a few well-informed and dedicated Stagehands, continued to fill speaking requests. In all, they spoke to some 15,940 persons in 82 speaking engagements. But no formal emphasis on a permanent speakers' bureau was made by the theatre at that time.

In 1964, with training needed for new Stagehands, a kit of background and season information was prepared for the ticket-drive workers. This kit was bolstered with additional specialized material and used as a working tool for speakers. The ticket-drive workers were urged to solicit speaking engagements, and were given forms to note speaking possibilities. These were passed on to a volunteer speakers' chairman who filled the requests from The Stagehands' members or the theatre staff. Using the film, "Miracle in Minnesota," which was first available in 1964, we were able to set up a "Guthrie Theatre" program consisting of speaker, film showing, and question period.

The pattern repeated itself. After the drive was over, speaking requests continued. Again, staff and volunteers carried out their assignments with notable results. During 1964, some 236 speaking engagements, of which 52 were at schools, were filled. In all, some 35,806 persons were reached, more than double the previous year. We realized the staff and a few volunteers could no longer carry the burden without help. In 1965 the decision was made to form a permanent, year-round, volunteer speakers' bureau. We wanted the majority of talks to be given by volunteers who, as members of the community, would be speaking to their peers. Their enthusiasm would not be suspect, especially by groups who were not theatre-oriented, while a theatre staff member might be considered to be just "doing his job" of selling the theatre.

In 1964 we had brought the speakers together before the ticket drive and numbed them with an all-day meeting that was practically a short course in theatre, administration, and public relations. Wisely, in 1965 we condensed our material and shortened the training program to a two-hour evening meeting. A more comprehensive kit, emphasizing the season's plays rather than the theatre, was compiled exclusively for speakers.

A new element was added. Dr. Arthur Ballet—a recognized authority on drama from the University of Minnesota's Department of Theatre Arts, and a fearless, witty speaker—was hired to tell the speakers about the season's plays. He had, on his own initiative, prepared mimeographed historical and critical backgrounds on the plays to give the speakers. We, in turn, had rushed completion of the guide to the season's plays, "Setting the Stage," and it was ready for the speakers. Dr. Ballet's talk had been taped and speakers, learning of its existence, were soon asking to borrow the tape when they gave their talks, and to use excerpts that were particularly witty or enlightening. We made dubs, and learned our lesson. In 1966 banded records of Dr. Ballet's season talk were hastily pressed and given to each speaker. The record became a prized "collector's item," with the speakers considering it a personal gift from the theatre for their services.

From our 1965 experience we concluded that an active, year-round, volunteer speaker's organization demanded a full-time staff member to service it. No volunteer could give the necessary time, or have the necessary day-to-day knowledge of theatre policy and events, adequately to arrange and service speaking engagements. If speaking requests are to be sought and serviced adequately, the staff coordinator will have to give much more than 40 hours a week in time and effort. Through The Stagehands, and by circulating a brochure describing the services of the speakers' bureau, we committed the theatre to this community service. We suggested a program of talks on the season's plays, film showings, and tours of the theatre. Backstage tours, incidentally, proved an exceptionally effective way of more deeply involving audience and potential audience with the theatre. When they could learn for themselves the complexities of the backstage operation and meet the people who made it work, they felt closer to the Minnesota Theatre Company. It was more *our* theatre, not just *the* theatre. Tours were arranged at all times of the year, and with the help of trained guides from The Stagehands and the ushers, some 15,000 people a year learned about the inner workings of the theatre.

The technical organization of a speakers' bureau can best be tailored by each institution to fit its unique needs and community. A few factors we learned are:

1. Accurate records of each talk should be kept. They comprise an invaluable contact list for group sales efforts.

2. The speakers' coordinator should gather all additional information possible about the requesting group—such as previous attendance by the group, previous speakers, ethnic background, knowledge of theatre per se, taboos, strong interests—and pass this information to the speaker well in advance of his talk.

3. Coordination of tours, scheduling of film, and other details are best handled by a staff coordinator rather than by a volunteer.

4. A reminder call *must* be made to the speaker 24 hours before the engagement, with final details repeated.

5. Follow-up calls to the group should be made by the volunteer chairman, again speaking as a member of the community. As a volunteer and not a staff member, the chairman will get a more honest report of the group attitude. If that attitude is receptive, the chairman can then notify staff members who should then query the group on the possibilities of their attendance. These follow-up calls also help to weed out inept volunteer speakers and are an opportune way of answering any further questions which may have arisen.

6. A mid-season meeting is advisable to answer questions the speakers are having difficulty with, to pass out new promotional material such as critical quotes, and to keep the theatre in personal touch with the speakers. The cost of a speakers' bureau is nominal when compared with its value. In addition to volunteer help, administration of the program took no more than one-quarter of one staff person's time. All direct expenses

—such as office supplies, postage stamps, travel, and production of the recording—came to about $1,200. The theatre asked no speaking fees for its personnel, and no fees were asked for volunteer appearances. The film also was free, although we asked the requesting group to furnish a projector and, whenever possible, someone to run it. If an organization volunteered a speaker's fee, it was accepted with the understanding that it would go into the needy-students' fund of the theatre.

One exception was made to the no-fee rule. If a group requested a technical talk on a specific field, a small fee would be asked. Actors speaking about the theatre did not usually receive a fee, but if an honorarium was offered, it was accepted for their personal use.

While a great deal of this chapter concerns volunteer speakers, it must clearly be stated that, when it came to public speaking, the entire staff and company at the Guthrie Theatre were cooperative, willing and effective. To defray expenses and keep the staff from constant traveling, we asked that groups outside a 100-mile radius pay travel and living expenses. Usually staff members were asked to fill out-of-state engagements because of the additional promotional work done in each town. When an out-of-state request was received, we would suggest that the requesting group contact other community organizations for a joint meeting. The group benefited because costs of the speaker's trip could then be shared, and the theatre benefited by reaching a larger audience and involving more of the community. Most importantly, we found our speakers were getting the opportunity of talking to groups which would otherwise never have considered inviting a speaker on theatre. The theatre was making personal contact with some Noes.

For crisis occasions, such as the Cedar Rapids AAUW, we would call on out-of-state Stagehands, board members, or friends of the theatre such as Don Tescher or Dr. Ballet, often with unexpected results. On one occasion, Dr. Ballet filled in at the last minute for an ill Oliver Rea in Omaha. Ballet hilariously reported the next day that he was now "Oliver Rea" in Omaha, despite his attempts at explanation. He was particularily amused by one little old lady who kept insisting: "Really, Mr. Rea, you don't look a *bit* like your picture!"

Speakers going out-of-state were asked to make community calls on the Chamber of Commerce, the librarian, the high-school principal, the press, and the arts organizations. The organization originally requesting the speaker was asked to contact the local schools and colleges, enabling the speaker to address the students and to show the film. If the speaker's schedule permitted, we would often contact neighboring towns to arrange a speaking schedule in their community on the same trip.

One such rewarding trip came from a request to have Morison speak to a Duluth organization. We had been planning to organize a Stagehands chapter in that city, and so contacted the two Duluth board members, Maury Cohen and Mrs. William Van Evera. We asked them to have a meeting of key women in the area meet with the two of us and set up a Stagehands group. Could they line up any additional speaking engagements? They certainly could! In two days, we filled seven separate speaking engagements at schools and civic organizations (Morison drove 70 miles to speak in a neighboring town), five joint appearances, had five appointments with civic leaders, showed the film four times, made three radio and television appearances not including press interviews and attended three cocktail parties and two dinners.

The results of the two days' work in Duluth were a good example of the effectiveness of what we called "root digging"— efforts to establish firm roots for the theatre community. A Stagehands group was established, complete with directing committee and 150 members encompassing Duluth and her sister city, Superior, Wisconsin. Initial contacts were made toward the establishment of a ticket agency. An exploratory luncheon with high-school English and drama teachers from the area resulted in bus-loads of students traveling 160 miles one-way to the theatre; two board members were convinced of their value and usefulness; our contacts with the news media were strengthened, and Duluth was made keenly aware of the Guthrie Theatre. We also acquired a cold (Morison) and a frost-bitten ear (Fliehr).

This example explains why our policy was never to refuse a speaking request, whether it involved 6 or 600 people.

From all such speaking and contact with potential audiences, we were learning a number of valuable things. The theatre was speaking primarily to groups of Yeses and Maybes. Occasionally, when speakers were forced upon one organization in a town by another which hoped to defray expenses, the theatre also reached some Noes.

The content of the speeches varied considerably depending upon the category of the group. We were just as eager to speak to Yeses already attending the theatre as to Maybes and Noes, because it gave us a chance to increase their theatrical knowledgeability, ultimately developing a more challenging and critical audience. Speeches to such groups were usually made by top people from the artistic or production staffs or by members of the company, and dealt with a wide variety of subjects on the theatrical arts and dramatic literature. With Maybes, the speech usually dealt with the plays of the season, the goals and objectives of the theatre, or its backstage workings—an attempt to make the theatre and what it was presenting more familiar and less formidable. Generally the speeches were not hard sell, but, we hoped, stimulating and educational lectures.

The Noes presented a more challenging problem. It was in talking with them and answering their questions that we began to feel they were not a hopeless cause, as we had first thought. And we began to get a clue as to how they could be reached. On one occasion, Morison faced the disinterested members of a men's club who were tolerating his presence only because the local AAUW had exerted its feminine influence and arranged his appearance. He was introduced with the comment, "We don't usually have speakers on culture and philosophy things. We're more baseball types." Quaking, Morison began by asking the group to try to imagine what it would be like to be the *only* fan at a final World Series game. They understood that much of the excitement would be missing without the interaction of crowds and players. He then made the analogy with live theatre and launched into an explanation of why theatre was not merely a poor substitute for movies and television, but a separate medium, important and exciting in their society. The question session that followed was long and illuminating. Four weeks later, a busload of those men and their wives came to a performance. The baseball talk, with variations, became the "Why Bother With Theatre?" speech and was often repeated.

We were learning about the Noes. They had been intimidated by culture and theatre. They had no intention of ever setting foot in the Guthrie Theatre. It simply was not, in their opinion, of any importance or concern to them. They didn't read about the theatre or listen to anything about it or think about it. Nothing we could do by normal channels of communication would ever bring them to it. The Cultural Curtain was drawn. But when we went to the Noes, when we encountered them on their home grounds and placed theatre *in terms relevant to their interests and their lives,* then we could begin to part the curtain. We could begin to chip away at the formidable wall of fear—fear of the arts ingrained by generations of intimidation.

We had found that diligent exploration of a community could make new friends, strengthen existing contacts, publicize the organization through local media, and keep the staff informed of the community's attitudes, complaints, and expectations. Speaking engagements can be person-to-person contact in its purest sense, or they can merely be a necessary drudgery. Whether such engagements are meaningful and valuable depends on the staff attitude and management policy. We recommend the "root digging" speaking engagement as indispensable in any program of audience development. As a result of such "root digging," first the individuals come to the theatre, then the small groups spurred by local word of mouth, then the busloads. And, gradually, the organization gains staunch, working supporters in every community, "volunteers" who will respond enthusiastically to any call for aid, information, or assistance. In other words, from the person-to-person contact made by speaking comes audience, fans, friends, and ultimately the dedicated personal salesmen who will make new person-to-person contacts.

Chapter 20

Speakers' Aids

It was smoky and hot in the projection room, and Oliver Rea was edgy with tension. For almost 25 minutes he'd been watching the first screening of the film about the Guthrie Theatre for which he had promoted a sizeable grant from the Ford Foundation. The board members and staff seated around him were carefully unresponsive.

Shooting on the film had begun in September of 1963, and now, in January of the next year, they were seeing the results of months of work, weeks of cables and cameras and sound booms interfering with the normal business of the theatre, and some $35,000 in cold, hard cash. The final credits flashed on the screen, the lights went up, and Rea looked around him. "Well," he said with forced heartiness, "what do you think of it?"

From the chorus of the expected trite comments of "Great," "Fine piece of technical work," and "Very interesting," two voices caught his attention. "It'll do the job it's supposed to do," and the skeptical answering mutter: "Yeah, but it sure won't win any awards!"

The 25-minute, 16-millimeter sound-color film, "Miracle in Minnesota," became the prime selling and educational tool of the Minnesota Theatre Company. By 1966 14 prints had been worn out from showing throughout the United States to more than 240,000 adults, plus about 97,000 students. The USIA translated it and circulates prints in 40 foreign countries. Every summer the University of Wisconsin shows it three times weekly for nine weeks to its Extension Department's School for Workers—groups of union and labor leaders from all over the country. Libraries and colleges are adding it to their permanent files; colleges and high schools request it each year to show to incoming freshmen; theatres and theatre committees use it in fund drives; drama departments use it in teaching sessions; and community organizations request its return at regular intervals. It has won three national awards.

Written by Morison and produced by Empire Photosound, Inc. of Minneapolis, its purpose was to document the story of the creation of the Tyrone Guthrie Theatre, and to demonstrate what this concept of professional, classic, repertory theatre was all about. It was designed as a tool to help speakers tell the story of the theatre, its history and goals, and to communicate the excitement of living theatre. But the film was only one of such speakers' aids we instituted.

As we were committed to a speaking program on a massive scale, it was evident that the theatre would not be able to furnish speakers of Guthrie's eloquence on every occasion. Having to rely on many speakers of varying ability, we concluded that well-done audiovisual aids were absolutely essential. Industry knows that it must equip its salesmen with various kinds of printed and audio-visual sales tools. The arts can well heed the lesson!

The first such sales tool used by the theatre was a recording prepared for the initial season-ticket drive. Since the company and artistic staff were not present when the drive began —and would be tied up with rehearsals when they did arrive— they obviously could not attend meetings to help explain what the theatre was about. With the entire concept of the theatre still in limbo, it seemed wise to do everything possible to assist available speakers and The Stagehands in their difficult task of trying to explain that intangible, the coming season. The answer was obvious: Bring the artistic staff and company to the coffee parties via recording.

A 12-inch, 33–1/3 LP record, narrated by Dave Moore, popular WCCO-TV newscaster, was prepared. Within the narrative framework were the voices of Tyrone Guthrie, Douglas Campbell, Hume Cronyn and Jessica Tandy (via radiophone from the Caribbean), George Grizzard, and Rita Gam—each explaining what the theatre would be and why it was important and exciting. At the end of the record, *Music Man* Robert Preston urged the citizens of the Midwest to attend this new, exciting theatre. Some 600 copies of the record were used by The Stagehands and other speakers during the 1963 season-ticket drive.

When "Miracle in Minnesota" became available for the season-ticket campaign of 1964, we allocated three prints for exclusive use by The Stagehands and made a projector available. The volunteers picked up the film and projector and returned them to the office after each showing. Experience proved this method to be cumbersome, however; consequently, in 1965 we rented three continuous self-feed projectors which were easier for volunteers to use.

Originally, no charge was made for use of the film except for shipping. With increased demand, we tried to limit its use to the five-state area by asking a two-dollar rental charge from outside that region. Earlier we had made the choice between handling the film through the theatre office and placing it with a film-distribution firm. Distributing firms must charge a fee for each booking regardless of the area served or type of organization requesting the film. We felt this fee would limit usage in our primary area and because the film was an invaluable selling tool, we wished to gain the largest possible distribution by offering the film as a service to the community rather than making it a purchased privilege. Also, we wanted to maintain personal contact with every organization that requested the film. We wanted to be in a position to offer a speaker to present the film, a tour of the theatre, or better yet, to suggest that the requesting group make a trip to see an actual performance at the theatre.

With the success of "Miracle in Minnesota" as a speakers' aid and sales tool, we began to look for ways to expand the audiovisual library. In 1964 KTCA-TV, the Twin Cities' educational television channel, had presented a program on the open stage, featuring Douglas Campbell and Professor David Jones, then of the University of Minnesota. The program was videotaped and was a fascinating comparison of platform and proscenium stages and their history. We made a film transfer from the videotape and prepared a 25-minute, black-and-white film called "The Open Stage" to be used primarily for groups of Yeses who were relatively knowledgeable about theatre.

As theatre interest in the area matured, requests for presentations on the various technical aspects of play production increased. The production staff obviously could not handle all such requests. In discussions with our Educational Advisory Council and other educators, the need for audiovisual materials related to these areas of theatre was repeatedly stressed. We thought of filmstrips and decided to prepare a series on technical aspects of the theatre arts. The initial project, a filmstrip on costuming, was assigned to The Stagehands' special projects division, scheduled for distribution in 1967. We were also working on preparation of taped excerpts from a series of radio programs produced by WLOL-FM, called "Backstage at the Guthrie," to be made available to high schools and colleges. Many other similar projects were planned.

From our experience, we concluded that the possibilities for audiovisual aids are limited only by imagination, need, and money. They are so valuable that it would seem expedient to curtail other expenditures in order to probe more deeply into this field of educational service and audience development. The arts are audiovisual by nature. Obviously the best means of public enjoyment and appreciation is to experience the arts in actual performance or at a gallery. But convincing the public that they should so participate is difficult, especially when either the printed or spoken word is used exclusively. If, because of psychological barriers and the ever-present Cultural Curtain, it is impossible to get a large portion of the population to sample the arts on their own initiative, the most potent way to interest them is to bring the artistic experience *to* them in any way possible. Let people participate in an artistic experience in their own familiar surroundings and in terms meaningful to them, and the arts will begin to chip away at the rigid barriers which keep them from seeking out the artistic experience.

Our own experience leads us to conclude that the field of audio-visual materials is an enormously important one which the arts have tended to ignore as promotional media. We question whether considerably more emphasis should not be put on the creation of imaginative and dynamic films, filmstrips, tapes and records which can be taken to people who are not yet motivated to bring themselves to the arts. Plans should be made for producing and using such audio-visual presentations which stress the special excitement the arts can bring to contemporary life.

By 1964 we had come to the conclusion that the person-to-person contact of our Speaker program augmented by audio-visual materials, was an extremely valuable technique for audience development. We knew also that we must have ever-widening circles of dedicated evangelists to help us. We needed to make more good friends to accomplish this. It took a bit more time before we discovered the secret of how an institution really makes friends.

Chapter 21

What Can We Do for You?

It was 3:30 A.M. on an August day in 1963. The place was Waterloo, Iowa. Douglas Campbell was again running through his repertoire of salty stories and bawdy English ballads, this time at a private party for members of the Waterloo Community Theatre. Allan Longacre, the theatre's full-time director, looked on happily. "This," he said, "is the most important thing that has ever happened to the Waterloo Community Theatre. We'll no longer be looked upon as those peculiar kooks who put on plays, because finally someone important has paid attention to us." That day in Waterloo had begun at lunch with several Waterloo citizens interested in the theatre who had gathered at Morison's request, made through the editor of the town newspaper.

Campbell had taken an immediate liking to Longacre and their conversation had roamed widely from the state of American professional theatre to the plight of that local amateur group playing in a 65 seat house —located in the basement of an old school house on the wrong side of the Waterloo tracks—which was called "Theatre in Your Lap." Finally, Campbell's fist came down on the table with a shuddering whack. "All right, let's get down to business," he said with

Shakespearean impressiveness. "What can we do for you?"

Longacre didn't hesitate. "If I can organize a party for all the members of our theatre tonight, will you come?"

"What can we do for you?" became the six most important words in the vocabulary of the Minnesota Theatre Company's Public Relations Department, and the lesson was learned at Waterloo.

It could just as well have been learned by listening carefully that same August as Jessica Tandy, portraying Linda Loman in *Death of a Salesman,* said of Willy, "Attention must be paid." You cannot expect anyone to pay attention to you unless you first pay attention to them.

The cynic will scoff at the apparent altruism of an audience-development philosophy based on "what can we do for you?" and may wink knowingly when it is acknowledged that the Waterloo, Iowa, Community Theatre now organizes annual bus trips to the Guthrie Theatre in Minneapolis. But there is more to the philosophy than selling tickets. We had begun to realize that the theatre was somehow more than the traditional Broadway theatrical enterprise. It was, in a sense, community property. Our responsibility was more than just selling tickets. It was opening new doors to the theatrical experience for new people. To accomplish that end the theatre needed friends. Friends do not result from slick public relations or press agentry; they are made in direct proportion to the genuineness with which an institution says to its community, "What can we do for you?" Some months after Waterloo, Campbell summed it up: "When you give something of importance to every part of your community, the community will not let you fail."

We began deliberately to look for ways to give something of importance to every part of our community, whether there were audience prospects or not. There had been talk of "serving the community" from the beginning, but the original concept of service was mainly confined to the primary purpose of any theatre—presenting the best possible productions of great plays—and someday to sending touring companies to towns in the area. But we began to wonder whether performing plays in the Tyrone Guthrie Theatre to four or five percent of the population could truly be called *community* service. Would this develop the broad base of general moral, financial, political, and audience support which would guarantee the theatre's stability and success? Would such a limited concept of service really create the proper climate in which the institution could fulfill its promise? Our experience with the Minneapolis City Tax Assessor didn't make us feel very comfortable about the answer.

As the months went by, we and our colleagues came to the conclusion that we had better begin to think of the theatre as a community resource which every part of the community should be encouraged to draw upon, much like a library. The theatre, we believed, had to accept the responsibility which comes with the privilege of membership in a community by demonstrating its willingness to be of service to all parts of its community. We were convinced that in so doing we would also be opening the doors to the theatrical experience for parts of that community which would otherwise never have attended Minnesota Theatre Company performances.

Any community is a kind of colorful, interlocking mosaic which forms a total composition. It is composed of art and cultural organizations; libraries, schools, and churches; state and local political institutions; charitable and civic organizations, labor unions, industry, business and commerce, and many more interest groups. How can a theatre serve each part of this community? The answers could come only from person-to-person dialogues.

One of the first of our dialogues began that day in Waterloo—a dialogue which ripened into friendship with the community theatres of the area. Originally there had been some resentment and fear among community theatres about the Guthrie Theatre "moving in" on their territory. But as we moved from town to town, evincing genuine interest in what community theatres were doing and asking how we could be of help, suspicion began to turn into acceptance and finally into cooperation.

The most frequent request was for assistance in promotion and public relations. In this area we could be of some help to our own advantage as well. A community theatre is the local salesman for living theatre. It was evident that no person from Waterloo was going to travel 275 miles to the Guthrie Theatre unless he had enough basic interest in drama to have attended or participated in the theatre in his own town. Therefore, whatever we could do to help community theatres to enlarge and broaden their own audiences would eventually enlarge and broaden the Minnesota Theatre Company audiences.

The dialogues resulted in the regular participation of members of the company and staff in state and regional community-theatre meetings, the providing of some specific help on promotional problems to individual theatres, and finally in the conducting of a one-day workshop held in the Twin Cities called "In Quest of Audience." Open to all theatre people in the Midwest, the workshop was dedicated to "the exchange of ideas on public relations and promotion philosophy and the creative application of professional sales and marketing principles to the development of new audiences for the arts."

From 10:00 A.M. to 6:00 P.M. on October 24, 1964, more than 100 representatives from 70 theatres heard professionals from theatre, advertising, public relations, management, and media talk, explain, discuss, and answer questions. The conference was a success. It led to closer understanding and joint efforts among all theatres in the area. The participants wanted another such workshop session, and plans for a second "In Quest of Audience" were made—and then reluctantly filed away. The twin bugaboos of time and money had interfered again. But another organization, the recently-established Region VII office of ANTA, offered to help by organizing and sponsoring a similar meeting, this time on administration and funding, which was well-attended and appreciated by the theatre representatives. (A report of the meeting is available from ANTA Region VII office.)

Another dialogue, this time with the educational community, began in 1963 with the initiation of a program for high school students to attend performances. This program was later expanded by the formal appointment of an Educational

Advisory Council. This program will be dealt with in a later section.

The public libraries, an important part of any community, were the next concern. For our 1965 season, we had printed a study guide called "Setting the Stage" which contained background information on the five plays of our season. Hannis Smith, head of the library division of the State Department of Education, was contacted. If we made complimentary copies of our guide available to all public libraries in the state, would he distribute them through his office? He not only distributed them but suggested we write the heads of library departments in all our surrounding states, offering them the same material. "And," he added, "tell them you send out speakers and the movie to help them with their adult education programs." We were beginning to learn about libraries. One of their problems is organizing programs to get more people into and using the libraries. The response to our mailing was a flood of requests from libraries in five states asking for speakers, display materials, programs of readings, the film—anything they could use in their programs to make the libraries more exciting and more appealing. We complied with every resource we could muster, and the libraries of the five states began to become focal points for background and information on the Guthrie Theatre.

We shared what we were learning about libraries with other cultural institutions and in 1966, at a state meeting of library adult-program directors, every major cultural institution was invited to send a top representative to tell the libraries how they could help. In turn, the librarians told the cultural organizations what their citizens wanted and needed. Without exception, the arts groups offered to help. The surface was just being scratched concerning ways in which theatre—and all other cultural institutions—and public libraries could be of mutual help. It was even suggested at the 1966 meeting that public libraries might some day serve as ticket outlets for the performing arts!

We turned to another area. How can a theatre serve the religious community? The question had puzzled us. Some clergymen believe that drama is an important moral force and use it for that purpose. There is a larger number who are more inclined to think of theatre simply as "show biz," however. Still others consider the theatre as sinful. There must be a way, we thought, to make the theatre more important and meaningful to all clergymen in their work.

We gathered a group representing all faiths and asked, How can we help you? Out of the first meetings with this group came a proposal for a one-day symposium for clergymen at the Guthrie Theatre, at which we would trace the historical relationship of religion and theatre and discuss ways in which drama could be valuable in the presentation of contemporary religious problems. The plan for this conference lies mouldering in the files, locked in by lack of time and money. But despite our failure to initiate a symposium on religion and drama, we continued our dialogue with the church community, and slowly some of their needs became apparent. Two churches, Zion Baptist and Judson Memorial Baptist, wanted to present a drama using their young-people's groups, illuminating for their congregations the racial tensions that exist in Minnesota. One church had a Negro congregation, the other a white. Both churches turned to the Minnesota Theatre Company for help in finding the right play. Martin Bard, then serving with the company under the Ford administrative intern program, offered to help.

In ensuing meetings, Bard and people from the two churches evolved the Zion-Judson Docudrama Players, teenagers without previous stage experience who created and performed a program of sketches on racial incidents in the state which had been taken from actual news reports. First performances were for the congregations, with discussion sessions following each performance. The impact was electrifying. Excitement could not be contained and soon the group was performing by request for other civic and religious organizations throughout the Twin Cities. They were also asked to perform at a session of the Congress of the National Methodist Board of Missions in Chicago. The Guthrie Theatre had found another way to serve.

Another call came in mid-1966, this one from the Greater Minneapolis Council of Churches. Would the theatre be interested in working with it on a program of Bible readings to illustrate the Bible as beautiful literature? Our answer was yes. From this call plans were begun, but never brought to fruition, for a major production involving the Minnesota Theatre Company, portions of the Minneapolis Symphony Orchestra, and a choir. The product was to be built around Bible readings which have to do with man's search for freedom, and was to be presented in 1967 for limited performances on otherwise dark nights at the Guthrie Theatre. Plans were to then scale it down so that three or four actors could perform it at churches in the area, using the local church choir and musicians.

In so serving the religious community, the Guthrie Theatre hoped to achieve another way of reaching the Noes. People who had heretofore thought theatre could not be important in their lives could have been exposed to theatrical experience about something which *was* important to them, the Bible, in surroundings which were comfortably familiar—their own church. We believe that many in those audiences would have come away with a different feeling about drama in general and about the Minnesota Theatre Company in particular. It is likely that at least those people would have moved another step closer to being Maybes.

The ways in which theatre might serve industry—by helping in employee recruitment, for instance—and business—by helping with projects to attract conventions or tourists—are perhaps obvious, but we did not pursue dialogues in these connections to their fullest. We did, however, rise to the challenge of how a theatre can better serve the trade-union community. We began that dialogue several years ago with Jim Jones, editor of the Minneapolis *Labor Review*. In the summer of 1966, a meeting was held of six members of diverse unions picked by Jones. These union members and their wives attended a performance and an informal supper with several members of the theatre staff and company which was given after the play at Douglas Campbell's home. The question for discussion: What can the theatre do to help you with your problems? The discussions ranged far and wide, shedding a great deal of light on the reasons why many union members shy away from any contact with the arts and culture.

One problem uncovered was particularly interesting because of its bearing on the concept of service. A problem shared by all unions, the union leaders told us, is getting good attendance at meetings. There were discussions about whether the theatre could develop a short program of readings and entertainment to be presented at union meetings—a program designed not only to attract members to meetings, but also to familiarize them with the Guthrie Theatre and its company. The possibilities were placed under investigation.

Another union possibility recently interested us. The leader of one of the largest unions in the Twin Cities said that he had a very difficult time getting his 600–700 union stewards to regular meetings. Most of them had never been to the Guthrie Theatre for a performance, and probably never would go, partly because they were intimidated by the building and its surroundings. Yet he felt they were all curious enough about it so that if his union-steward meeting was held *in* the theatre he would get excellent attendance. Could his stewards meet in the theatre, and could the theatre present a short program before the meeting, explaining the building itself and what the company did in it? Plans for such a meeting in 1967 were being discussed when the authors left the Guthrie Theatre.

Such a plan, if executed, could be of service in helping unions to increase meeting attendance, and an important group of Noes can be reached. Members of the labor force are often intimidated by theatres, and by drawing them to the building on a different pretext, they can become more familiar and more comfortable in the surroundings.

The list of community dialogues which we started and didn't continue, and those which we should have started but didn't, is long and unnecessary here, for the examples presented hopefully communicate the idea we are presenting.

In our opinion this is the most important concept to come out of our experience. Find a way to be of service to every part of the community and the community will not let you fail. This is the key in providing the proper climate within a community so that an artistic institution can flourish and develop every kind of support from all parts of the community. This is the way to make something which is strange familiar to those people who let strangeness keep them from participation. This is one important way to create an environment within the community conducive to the full growth and free expression of the institution.

Chapter 22

A Matter of Manners

"An invitation from the Tyrone Guthrie Theatre to attend a press luncheon at the Sheraton Ritz Hotel in Minneapolis last Saturday noon, proved to be an interesting experience. The reason for the press luncheon was to tell the story of next season's plays and players. The invitation was extended to members of the press and radio, and their wives."

The writer was Mrs. John Harmon, wife of the editor and publisher of the Litchfield (weekly) Independent Review, reporting in her column "On the Home Front" on Thursday, September 24, 1964. She continued:

"This wife was pleased with the invitation, but husband, John, who considers himself very much of an outdoor man, was not so sure that this close contact with the Arts was exactly his type of thing—it might be boring. Besides, the Shrine Rodeo was on in St. Paul, and being both a Shriner and a horseman, he much preferred going to that. So we "compromised" and went to the noon luncheon, then to the Guthrie Theatre for the matinee performance of Volpone, on to a quick dinner, and over to the Shrine Rodeo at 7:30—a full day.

"Although we felt ill at ease and much like coun-

try bumpkins when we walked into the Cotillion Room where the luncheon was held, knowing not another person there, the friendly welcome by Miss Ann Richards, public relations assistant for the Guthrie Theatre, soon put us at ease. In a very short time we were visiting with so many friendly folks, not only from the metropolitan press, but from small rural areas like our own. We like to think that our local weekly paper is every bit as important to the people as the large dailies, but in a different and much more personal way. We feel we are the "grass roots," so to speak. The Theatre Company presumably goes along with this thinking, or they would not have felt it important to tell their story to us. . . .

After we were back home, comments from the male side of the family ran like this, "You know, I have an altogether different feeling about the Guthrie Theatre now. I think I'd like to see another one of their plays."

It is possible that attending the performance of *Volpone* may have made Mr. and Mrs. John Harmon merely *fans* of the Tyrone Guthrie Theatre; it is equally possible that something as basic as "the friendly welcome by Miss Ann Richards" made them *friends*.

Nobody can look upon an institution as a friend until that institution has come alive in terms of the human warmth of the people who comprise it. In the Twin Cities area, for example, the Minneapolis *Star* and *Tribune* enjoyed their greatest growth in both prestige and circulation during the decade after World War II. At that time nearly every major columnist, reporter, and editor was roaming the upper Midwest from one corner to the other, speaking, mixing, mingling—translating the meaning of an institution into the warm, flesh-and-blood terms of real human beings which comprised the institution. Similarly, WCCO, which now captures more than half of the area's radio audience, has for years had its on-the-air personalities spending almost as much time on the banquet circuit and riding in small-town festival parades as they spend on the air.

The task of winning friends for any institution is probably most analogous to politics. Press coverage, formal announcements, and posters are necessary, but in the final analysis it is the street-corner meetings, the hand-shaking, baby-kissing, and doorbell-ringing that do the job. This concept had vaguely been with us at the Guthrie Theatre since the Morison Report, but it remained for Nathan Cohen, drama critic for the Toronto *Star*, to push us into a clarifying description of the philosophy. Driving in from the airport one spring day when Cohen had come to review our productions, he asked, "How do you define public relations as it applies to a theatre?" There was a long silence, then a few halting attempts at explanation, and finally a rather clearcut statement from Kay. "I suppose it's simply the application of good manners to the public conduct of an institution— just treating every member of the public as you would a good friend."

It seemed rather obvious at the time but, pursued in depth, the concept becomes more profound and serves as an illustrating guide to the conduct of public affairs for any institution, particularly those in the clothing of public or semi-public organizations. There are the obvious and normal courtesies of good manners: Say "please" and "thank you," be pleasant, dependable, prompt. Obvious and often neglected. We had recognized the need for promptness in correspondence, and initiated a policy of answering every letter the same day it was received. This policy broke down under the pressure of opening nights some months later, but whenever possible we adhered to this policy. But there are other less obvious aspects to the good manners of friendship that are equally appropriate in the relationship of a theatre to the individuals in its community. Which one of us, for instance, has not been taught that a part of good manners is being a good listener. In developing an audience it seems crucial to us that a theatre be a good listener. A theatre cannot be sensitive to the needs of the community unless it knows them, and it cannot know them unless it listens. A theatre can listen to its community through the same ever-widening circles of friends through which it speaks. Communication is a two-way proposition. From the board of directors, the women's volunteer organization, the advisory committees and councils.

the speakers' bureau, and, indeed, from the wandering members of staff and company should come a ceaseless flow of information about the community they have contacted. Such feedback is invaluable to management in feeling the pulse of the community, not just its likes and dislikes concerning a particular production, but a feel of its total wants and needs, strengths and weaknesses, problems and opportunities. We have concluded that half the value of Dr. Guthrie's visit to Cherokee, Iowa; or of Douglas Campbell's presence at a community theatre party; or of the appearance of our actors, designers, and stage managers in high schools, colleges, Kiwanis Clubs, and church basements from Wisconsin to Montana lies in what these emissaries heard and absorbed. But such emissaries must listen with honest interest rather than with the boredom of perfunctory duty. The superficial show of good manners will not make good friends.

This leads us to another bedrock component of friendship —honesty. It is a part of the good manners of friendship to confide in friends, to admit mistakes, to take blame and give credit where due, to trust friends to bear with us as we face our problems. And it is a part of the good manners of an institution to treat its friends in the same, honest manner. It was our policy in press releases and public utterances as well as in private conversations with members of the press, audience, and other friends to be as honest as possible: to make the theatre's yearly financial and attendance statements a matter of public record, to state publicly our goals and to admit when we failed to reach them, and to admit our fallibilities and to ask forbearance. In speech after speech the theatre's goals were outlined with regard to the company, its productions, and its service. The theatre tried to assess its accomplishments and admitted that its reach often far exceeded its grasp. On more than one occasion, both Dr. Guthrie and Douglas Campbell publicly admitted failure to achieve all they had hoped to achieve in certain productions. There is certainly no excuse in public relations for self-deprecation, but neither is there value in failing to be honest. Eventually the people you think are friends will find you out and you will lose them.

It is also part of good manners to warn your friends of

something imminent which will affect them. This, too, applies as much to an institution as to an individual. It would have been better had we been able to make sure that every single member of the Minnesota Theatre Company was aware in advance of what they eventually read in the papers. Our basic press-release mailing list included the members of the board, The Stagehands, and the Educational Advisory Council. The newsletter, "Green Room," was instituted primarily to let the subscribers know about things which affected them. The examples of the application of good manners and personal friendship to the good manners of public relations are almost endless. Let it suffice to mention one more: that of being accommodating. It is basic to the good manners of friendship that everything possible be done to accommodate a friend. A true friend never says "no" where it is possible to help, and neither should a theatre company. No matter what the request or from whom, it must be treated with concern and importance.

We tried to answer each request with the same degree of enthusiasm, whether it was a question from Howard Taubman of *The New York Times* or a search for information from a Boise, Idaho, high-school student writing a theme.

One of the best, single friends the Minnesota Theatre Company had was Sister Mary Angelita, B.V.M., of Our Lady of Peace High School in St. Paul. In 1966, among other activities, Sister Angelita organized all the private and public high-school students of the city to distribute Guthrie Theatre posters. In the same year she was responsible for bringing the annual convention of the National Catholic Theatre Association to the Twin Cities and the Guthrie Theatre. Nobody remembers *exactly* how the friendship began, but as Sister Angelita recalls it, she called unannounced and unknown during our first season to make a simple request for her students. Sister Angelita remembers being treated as if she were the most important single person in the life of the Minnesota Theatre Company. And so she was—as is everyone else who is truly interested in the theatre. For the good manners of friendship dictate that a full measure of importance be given to any and all—no matter what their position or their request.

Chapter 23

Rewards of Friendship

The businessman clutched his briefcase, waved his ticket at the airline attendant, and strode across the concrete of the Twin Cities Metropolitan Airport to his plane. Halfway up the steps of the plane's ramp, in the twilight of a summer day in 1965, he stopped suddenly, listened carefully, then continued up slowly until he encountered the stewardess.

"You know," he said, "if I weren't at the airport I'd swear I was hearing the Guthrie Theatre trumpets." The stewardess pointed down toward the end of the parking area where a United Airlines Caravelle was deplaning its passengers. At the bottom of the ramp were the three, golden heraldic trumpets, a trademark of the Guthrie Theatre, blowing the familiar fanfare as a welcome to the arriving guests.

"Well, I'll be darned," said the businessman. "I wasn't hearing things. What's going on?" The stewardess explained that the trumpets were welcoming a chartered plane-load of people who had flown from Chicago for the weekend under sponsorship of the Chicago Daily News to attend Minnesota Theatre Company performances.

"Well, I'll bet we see a picture of that in the morning paper tomorrow," he said, and he ducked into the

> *plane whistling an echo of the six familiar fanfare notes.*

There was, indeed, a picture in the Minneapolis *Morning Tribune*. It was something of an occasion when a Chicago newspaper would promote a trip to the Twin Cities, and the public relations department had sent the trumpeters to the airport to give the theatre's Chicago friends a dazzling welcome. The trumpets were also there to make sure that the local newspaper would cover the occasion, and with plenty of pictures. It was important that the people of Minnesota know that a plane-load of people had come all the way from Chicago specifically to attend their own Guthrie Theatre.

The Morison Report had pointed out the power of word-of-mouth and personal recommendation in connection with the theatre, and had recommended the creation of a hard core of dedicated personal salesmen for the theatre. As one way to stimulate this personal recommendation, it also suggested the extensive use of publicity to inform potential audiences about who attended the theatre and how much they liked it. Of course, publicizing the enthusiasm of friends is one of the oldest techniques of theatrical press agentry, and quoting the favorable comments of critics in advertising, direct mail, and press releases is standard practice. But there are many other techniques, some of which have not yet been explored. We took the fairly obvious method of informing the media of any celebrities attending the theatre one step further. When Hildegarde, a favorite entertainer with Midwest audiences, came to a performance of *Richard III*, the staff photographer was assigned to take her picture with Hume Cronyn. A print was made into an advertising mat and distributed exclusively to weekly and small daily newspapers in the area with excellent results. The mat of Minnesota Twins baseball players Harmon Killebrew and Johnny Klippstein served the same purpose.

In trying to increase the number of blue-collar workers in the audience we used a testimonial technique. We advertised in the classified section of the two labor newspapers asking for union members who had attended the Guthrie Theatre. We then interviewed them, took their pictures and ran a series of small ads featuring the testimonials in the labor press. Union readers learned that other union members went to the theatre and liked the experience.

One of our most successful methods of stimulating personal recommendation was to take pictures of groups attending the theatre for their home-town newspapers. The editor of a small-town paper could not justify carrying much copy about the Guthrie Theatre unless the material had a local angle. If he and his wife attended a performance, he would be justified in writing a column or a review. But other than invite him and his wife to be guests at a performance, we could do little to provide him with a local angle. Pictures of people from his community —taken backstage, in the lobby or chatting with an actor— were another matter. If our funds had permitted, we would have had a photographer cover every performance; as it was, we managed to cover probably half the performances, either with staff-photographer Marty Nordstrom, or with Rick Hinkie, a college student who worked part-time for the department. These men were assigned to find groups we knew were in attendance, select three or four of the members and set up an interesting photograph. The captioned prints were sent off to the local editor and almost invariably used. Such pictures demonstrated to readers of the local newspaper that their neighbors were going to the Guthrie Theatre. If their neighbors went, maybe they should go, too. In addition, these pictures served as a stimulant to conversation and personal recommendation.

"Say, Mary, I saw your picture in *The Record* last week. You looked great."

"Yes, Sam and I went up to the Guthrie with our bridge club and we really had a wonderful time."

"Oh, you did enjoy it? John and I haven't gone yet. Is it really good? I mean, did you understand it?"

"It was simply beautiful, Rita. We saw *The Cherry Orchard* and even Sam liked it. It really was one of the most moving things. Let me tell you about it. . . ."

Mary is off and running, and the circles widen, prodded by the tool of publicity.

We actually did very little to stimulate word-of-mouth advertising and to publicize the theatre's friends compared to what we now believe can be done in this area. It is an area ripe for creative thinking and ideas, particularly when it comes to using "thought leaders."

In every social group, no matter how small, there is a leader or "influential." What such a person does greatly affects what is acceptable for the rest of his group. These leaders are difficult to identify, but once isolated, they can be powerful influencing forces. It appears to us now that any time and money spent by the theatre to learn more about thought leaders, to try to isolate those who influence Maybe and No groups, and then to devise creative and effective ways of influencing them to influence others, would be resources wisely spent. In addition to the unofficial leaders of social groups, there are those in the community whose official business it is to know what is going on in the community—including the activities of an arts institution—but who often neglect to remain informed: state and local legislators, mayors, visitors-bureau personnel, and various business, industry, and civic leaders. But in planning any publicity campaign, it must be assumed that very few people will really read the printed publicity; in fact, it is safe to go on the assumption that nobody reads it at all. Therefore, it is crucial that everything important which has been published in the mass media be circulated in some especially attention-demanding form to key persons. This is essential in creating the proper climate for total community support including ticket sales, fund-raising, and favorable governmental action.

Our most successful effort in this area occurred at the end of our first season. We prepared a four-page, newspaper-size reprint of reviews and articles favorable to the theatre. This material was enclosed with a letter from Oliver Rea and Peter Zeisler reporting on what the theatre tried to do to serve the community, and sent to community leaders at every level—state legislators, mayors, executive directors of Chambers of Commerce, business and industry leaders, and others. The mailing proved so valuable in creating the proper climate for the institution that we see now that it should have gone to a broader list; more important, it should have become an annual project.

We have tried to indicate in this section that we believe

person-to-person contact is the most effective tool for enlarging and broadening audience. We have tried to demonstrate why we believe that creating an ever-widening circle of dedicated friends is the way to increase the amount of person-to-person contact. And we have tried to outline ways in which we think a theatre can increase its circles of friends. Obviously this is an ideal; no organization has the resources to carry through every idea to perfection. But, even lacking resources to pursue the ideal in its entirety, an organization can and must utilize the tools of publicity and merchandising to do all it can to stimulate its most powerful resource: the personal recommendation of good friends.

Part Six

Of Tickets and Attendance

This theatre is not so important to our customers that we can spare any effort to make buying tickets and attending the theatre as easy and pleasant as possible.

The Morison Report

Chapter 24

Two on the Aisle

Barton Emmet swung into his swivel chair and reached for the telephone to call Don Foster, general manager of the Seattle Washington Repertory Theatre. While he waited, Emmet reviewed the pros and cons of the friendly battle which was raging among members of the administrative staff that summer of 1964. The question: Whether to use a coupon-book system for season tickets in 1965.

Forcing subscribers to choose, six or seven months in advance, the dates they wanted to attend the season's four plays was cutting into season-ticket sales he had to admit. The subscribers were unhappy, and the complicated procedure went against the Morison Report's firm admonition to "make the purchase of tickets as easy and convenient as possible." On the other hand, Emmet was apprehensive at the vision of hordes of subscribers who had put off exchanging their coupons, suddenly descending upon him at the final performances, rightfully demanding seats. The Seattle Theatre had tried coupons during their 1963–1964 season; how had coupons worked out there?

Foster was now on the line and Emmet asked the key question. Foster sighed quietly. "Well, we tried every way we could think of to remind people to ex-

*change their coupons before the end of the season, but
there were so many still outstanding when we closed
that we finally decided we would have to hold over
five productions into next season to accommodate our
subscribers."*

The experience of the Seattle Repertory Theatre with season-
ticket coupons helped tip the scales against the adoption of a
similar system for the Minnesota Theatre Company's third season. Members of the staff who had argued for coupons had
done so on the grounds that the theatre was making it unneces-
sarily difficult for people to buy tickets. And they were right;
for many people, ordering tickets in April for four or five
performances, spread over a six-month period in a complicated
rolling repertory schedule, was too much trouble. Grumblings
had come from the box office which found itself inundated
with exchanges. Louder grumblings came from season subscribers as changes in personal plans made it necessary to exchange a pair of tickets three or four times. But the probable
public relations problems connected with unexchanged coupons seemed to outweigh the advantages of making it "as easy
as humanly possible" to buy tickets. The decision appeared
wise at the time, although the problems of date-picking for subscribers undoubtedly was one of the major reasons for the continuing decline in season-ticket sales. The theatre simply
wasn't making it as easy as humanly possible to buy tickets.

The theatre did try, however, to make *exchanges* as convenient as possible and so to ease the pain of date-picking. On
the theory that if you can't solve it, kid it, we printed a "Date-
Picker" mailing piece in 1965 giving both humorous and serious suggestions on ways to make decisions about theatre dates
easier. In addition, we sent all subscribers a mail-order exchange form designed to help eliminate trips to the box office.

In 1966 a "Twin Bill" was created to try to solve a number
of problems including date-picking. Under the plan a Summer
Bill of 14 weeks consisting of three plays in repertory was presented. The Fall Bill was another 14 weeks opening the week of
Labor Day, consisting of two *additional* plays plus two plays
continued from the Summer Bill. A schedule of performances

was published in advance for the Summer Bill only; subscribers had to pick dates only for the three summer plays. They received coupons for the two new Fall-Bill plays. In August, a Fall-Bill schedule was printed and mailed with a coupon-exchange blank to subscribers, who then picked the dates for the autumn months at a time closer to attendance.

At least that was the theory. The plans seemed to make no appreciable difference in season-ticket sales, but in operation it did prove interesting. Coupons were promptly exchanged and very few were unredeemed at the end of the season. Perhaps the concern about coupons had been too great.

From the beginning, the theatre had a very liberal exchange policy: any time up to 30 minutes before curtain. In fact, it proved too liberal and it was changed in 1966 to 24 hours. What was happening was this: A house would be sold out. People were told all that day that no tickets were available. Then last-minute exchanges would come rolling in. There would be empty seats, and people who had been turned down would hear about it. They didn't like it, and the theatre didn't like the empty seats. The theatre was forced to make the matter of ticket exchanges a little more difficult.

One major decision, made prior to the opening of the theatre, helped make ticket-buying easy for many people. Dayton's (the leading retail department store in the area, with stores in Minneapolis, St. Paul, two suburbs, and the city of Rochester) had opened a ticket office in May, 1962. Arrangements were made soon afterward for them to handle Minnesota Theatre Company tickets on a commission basis. In St. Paul, tickets were also handled through the ticket office of another department store, Field Schlick's. There was an obvious advantage to the customer in having more places where he could purchase tickets; but the major convenience of the Dayton's arrangement was that the ticket-buyer could charge to his Dayton's account. Dayton's charge list numbers in the hundreds of thousands and is scattered through our area of prime potential. When a customer could simply telephone Dayton's for tickets, have them mailed to his home and the cost billed to his account, ticket-buying became about as easy as it is possible to be. And the theatre's customers took advantage of the convenience: Nearly half of all Guthrie Theatre tickets were sold by Dayton's, according to Guthrie Theatre records.

The large sale through Dayton's represented a substantial payment by the theatre in commissions. We have often thought it might be wise to study the feasibility of the theatre setting up its own charge and billing system. Some theatres have tried it with varying degrees of success. Dayton's reports that the ticket office is maintained as a customer service, so it may well be that the theatre would find itself with a large increase in workload and no increase in net revenue from its own charge system. It does seem imperative to us, however, that—in these days of easy credit and multiple credit cards—a theatre have a charge-and-mail system for its customers, whether through the theatre, a department store, or a ticket agent.

Even if a customer does not wish to charge his tickets, he should have the opportunity to make reservations by telephone. The theatre's policy was to accept such telephone reservations, but with the condition that payment be received 48 hours in advance of curtain time, which condition made such reservations only a minor convenience. The theatre-goer either had to call far enough in advance so that a check could reach the theatre by mail, or he had to make an additional trip to the theatre two days ahead of time to secure his tickets.

Ideally, as in many off-Broadway theatres, it should be possible to phone for reservations and pay for tickets upon arrival at the performance. Perhaps someday a practical plan will be devised by which this policy can be implemented without too much loss of revenue from those who fail to claim their reservations. One possible solution may be to experiment with the airlines' practice of "overselling" flights. If a theatre could determine, from carefully controlled experiments and research, the average percentage of telephone reservations that are *not* picked up, it could then oversell a full house by that percentage, and, consequently, offer better telephone-reservation service to its customers without suffering losses in revenue.

In addition to being easy, ticket-buying must also be a pleasant experience, and the responsibility here is almost entirely in the hands of the box office staff. The public relations function of a box office cannot be overemphasized. For some people it is the first direct contact—and often the only contact —they have with representatives of the theatre. The impact upon theatre image of box office personnel is overwhelming, and, indeed, the box office of a theatre should be considered an extension of the public relations department. Our experience has often made us think that perhaps it should actually *be* so. To make ticket-buying pleasant requires the highest-caliber personnel with excellent public relations instincts, impeccable manners, and infinite patience. It requires also that there be sufficient personnel so that attention can be paid to the customer's every question and whim. Finally, it requires that box office personnel be kept thoroughly informed about every phase of the theatre's operation so they can answer the hundreds of thousands of questions they get each season. There is nothing more damaging to public relations than a prospective customer who calls with a question and gets either no answer or the wrong one.

The Guthrie Theatre was fortunate in having an outstanding box office staff headed first by Mrs. Pat Peterson and then Mrs. Peg Liebly, both of whom had a keen sense of public relations. There were, of course, weaknesses in the staff from time to time; and many times we felt the box office was substantially understaffed. Long waits in line or on the telephone, or hurried and superficial attention do not make ticket-buying pleasant and can discourage even the most devoted theatre-goer. We tried to keep the lines of communication open to the box office. One season we held a meeting with the staff to explain promotion plans, and we now feel that it would have been advisable, before tickets went on sale, to have had a similar day-long training session for box office staff, at which members of all departments (including representatives of the acting company) would brief them on the plays, the artistic concepts and the production plans, as well as the promotional and public relations plans. No salesman can operate without complete knowledge of the product he sells.

In our search for easier and simplifying methods of buying and selling tickets, we looked into one intriguing possibility. In working with IBM representatives on a joint mailing list and data system for Twin Cities cultural organizations, we began to discuss the feasibility of an electronic box office with seat locations programmed into computers instead of printed on tickets. Electronically this is possible and beginnings have already been made toward studying the possibilities for the Midwest. We were not alone in our curiosity about computerized ticket-selling, however; in early 1967 at least two firms in the New York area were beginning to put such systems into operation, with nationwide networks of box office locations planned. Such systems on both national and regional levels seem inevitable. But it appears important to us that performing arts organizations move with speed to investigate and adopt the modern electronic methods of today. It is necessary not only to make business practices more efficient, but also to make ticket-buying as easy and pleasant as possible. The customers will not wait very long for the performing arts to catch up with the rest of the world.

Chapter 25

A Sense of Occasion

It was the summer of 1962. "Good Old Minn" had been decided upon as a location for the new repertory theatre, fund-raising was almost completed, and ground had been broken. Other business had taken Tyrone Guthrie back to England, and Oliver Rea had joined him in London for a few days to make further plans for their project. As might be expected, the two men spent their evenings at London theatres.

On one such night their taxi brought them to a small, dimly lit theatre in a particularly dingy part of London. They pushed their way through an over-crowded, dark, and drab lobby; waited interminably for an usher; and were finally shown to their very tatty and uncomfortable seats.

As the already dim houselights faded, Guthrie leaned over to Rea. "Oliver," he said, "I don't care how good this performance is, I'm not going to enjoy it. There is simply no sense of occasion about coming to this theatre."

Everyone who attends a theatre anticipates the experience as something of an occasion. It is the theatre's obligation—and the particular duty of the public relations department—to make sure the theatre-goer finds his sense of occasion echoed

in the building itself. Unattractive environs can dash the theatre-goer's anticipation and lower his spirits even before the curtain rises, making the task of entertaining him needlessly
difficult. A theatre must provide an environment of comfort
and cleanliness and then go on from there to heighten the
sense of occasion.

Live musicians to signal the beginning of each act with a
fanfare were initiated by Dr. Guthrie, first at Stratford, Ontario, then in the Twin Cities, as a way to heighten the sense of
occasion. Such a small thing has remarkable success. The sight
and sound of the musicians standing on an outside balcony
with drum and three heraldic trumpets sending their call
across the park gardens in the twilight of a summer's evening
heightens the anticipation of even the most unenthusiastic
theatre-goer. Many a regular customer lingers at intermission
to hear the last fanfare blown in the lobby.

Aside from the trumpet fanfares, little new or startling
has been done at the Guthrie Theatre to add to the sense of
occasion. The theatre tried to meet the basic requirements of
cleanliness, attractiveness, and convenience as well as possible,
following the philosophy that the members of the audience are
guests of the theatre, and, because they are paying guests, there
is an even greater obligation to make their experience a pleasant one in every way. Although the Tyrone Guthrie Theatre is a
new facility which was built expressly for its purposes, there is
no reason to suppose it met every requirement for creating a
sense of occasion. When the theatre was being designed, it became apparent that there were not enough funds to build it as
planned. Consequently, about 20 feet were cut off the original
design for the back of the building. Guthrie, in his book *A New
Theatre*, comments on the the decision:

> We did query this [reduction of space], suggesting that
> the foyers and front-of-house arrangements, which seemed to
> be handsomely, but needlessly spacious, might at least share
> the cut in space. . . . All of us agreed to this decision [to
> cut backstage area only], but I now believe it was wrong. We
> should have insisted upon the reduction of space being more
> equitably divided between front and backstage, refused to ac-

cept less adequate workrooms and offices, risked the consequences.

Although we were very much aware of the inadequacies in the building's production and administrative facilities, and have lived intimately with some of them, we tend to disagree with Guthrie. The consequences may have been a more comfortable staff, but only at the expense of an uncomfortable audience.

If the front of the house area had been "needlessly spacious" or the present facilities truly adequate, we would agree with Guthrie that some of this might have been sacrificed for the backstage area. Actually, however, there are some serious deficiencies in the present audience space. The lobbies are uncomfortably jammed when 1,437 people invade them at intermission. Restroom facilities are inadequate and located in the basement. The members of the audience seated in the upper part of the theatre must make their way down two flights of stairs, through a starkly bare basement lobby with echoing concrete floors, stand in restroom lines, and then retrace the long path to the second floor—all in 10 minutes. To paraphrase Guthrie's London comment, no matter how good the second act is, an audience member is not going to enjoy it if he has been forced into this sort of an ordeal. Further, if a member of the audience wants a drink of water, there are precisely two water fountains in the entire public area of the building. And before the patron even enters the theatre, he has already been inconvenienced by inadequate parking facilities which are located long blocks away from the theatre and for which he has been asked to pay 50 cents to the Park Board which owns the lot.

The theatre staff tried to overcome the inhospitality of these inadequacies. For example, the theatre's Volkswagen bus was used by house manager Archie Sarazin as a shuttle between the parking lot and theatre before performances. As an extra courtesy, an usher was assigned to open car doors and greet theatre-goers who were dropped off at the theatre entrance. On rainy nights, a second usher was on hand with a huge black umbrella, and the shuttle bus was available after the performance as well to save rainy walks back to the parking lot.

All of the ushers were carefully selected and trained, chosen from junior and senior high-school classes, meticulously inspected for frayed cuffs or wrinkled trousers—and shaggy haircuts—before every performance.

The staff of ushers—like the box office staff—should be considered important in public relations. For some people, ushers are their only direct personal contact with the theatre. Sarazin understood this and indoctrinated his staff well. One season we conducted a training session for ushers, giving them thorough background on the aims and activities of the Public Relations Department as well as briefing them on many backstage aspects of the company. These sessions should have been held annually. Sarazin also had the ushers trained in "Wheelchairmanship" by representatives of the Sister Kenney Institute in Minneapolis. Their skill in taking those in wheelchairs out of cars, up and down steps, and into the auditorium was much appreciated by handicapped guests of the theatre.

At every performance, a staff member from the public relations department was "on duty" to assist the house manager and box office staff if problems arose, to greet known friends of the theatre personally, to note any housekeeping slips or temporary inconveniences, and generally to observe the audience. In addition, the seat locations of all visiting press or broadcast people and other VIP's were listed for each performance. It was the staff member's duty to seek out such people, welcome them, and offer the courtesies of showing them backstage, introducing them to company members, or supplying photos and additional information. This personal attention helped enormously in making many good friends for the theatre.

Programs and lobby displays contribute to the total sense of occasion in a theatre and should be considered in that way. We tried to have picture displays in the outer lobby create a growing sense of excitement for the theatre-goer and also communicate the season's graphic image. In 1966 special displays dealing with the history and previous productions of the season's five plays attracted the interest of the audience. Plans were made to provide glass cases where costumes and properties of past productions could be displayed, but funds for this purpose never became available to us.

One problem in public relations faced by all theatres—and which we were unable to solve—is that of the latecomer who arrives just as the auditorium door is clicking shut and who is met with the sad tale: "Sorry, we must ask you to wait until the end of the first scene before we can seat you." Even if the latecomer admits that his own carelessness made him tardy, he is still annoyed at having to wait.

It is, of course, discourteous to those who arrive on time either to start the performance late, or to let latecomers step on other people's feet during the opening scene of the play. The solution would seem to be to provide facilities for latecomers so that they may somehow see and hear what is going on until an appropriate time comes for them to be seated. The obvious answer is a closed-circuit television system, which is now being tried in some theatres. One fortunate theatre in St. Paul was designed with a large curtained glass window at the rear of the house. By opening the curtains, late arrivals were pacified by watching the play, even though excluded from the auditorium. Another possible solution might be a kind of "Hold Booth"—a closed in, darkened space in the back wall of the auditorium with a long window. Sound could be piped into the booth and latecomers could both see and hear the performance until the hold was over.

Theatres must find creative ways to increase the excitement and sense of occasion of theatre performances without increasing the snobbery and social image. Often in the past the social and fashionable glamor of the audience was relied upon to provide the sense of occasion. But if a larger and broader audience is to be attracted, theatres must find other means to achieve that end. They must provide the kinds of glamor, excitement, and sense of occasion which do not intimidate prospective audiences. Toward this end in 1966 we toyed with the possibilities of a number of "gala" performances with special entertainment or events held in addition to the play. We came close to a Fourth of July "gala," complete with band concert, hot dogs, and ice cream on the lawn across from the theatre. In 1965, on the occasion of the opening of *The Caucasian Chalk Circle*, the Public Relations Department had a preopening party for several hundred state editors and their wives. It was not a cocktail buffet in a posh hotel, but a Caucasian-style barbecue picnic held across from the theatre, with Greek musicians and costumed folk dancers entertaining. It was a smashing success and helpful to the theatre's image.

The problem of enhancing the theatre-going experience and of putting the audience in the best possible mood for the play (*without* creating the wrong image and frightening away large portions of the audience) needs for its solution only more imagination applied to it. Audiences will not keep coming if theatres do not do everything possible to make purchasing tickets and attending the theatre increasingly easy, pleasant and full of the sense of occasion.

Part Seven

Some Means to an End

This report does not attempt to suggest all of the means by which the end may be accomplished. But it provides a framework within which any pertinent technique can be used. We should not waste time with efforts which do not contribute to this strategy just because "that's the way it's always been done."

The Morison Report

Chapter 26

Advertising and
Advertising Agencies

Sunday, September 11, 1966, Minneapolis Tribune.

The Morison Report did not contain a section on newspaper advertising, and the use of newspaper space was only mentioned in passing in connection with the schedule for the first season ticket drive. But the decision had to be made early as to what role ads in the daily press would play toward accomplishing the total strategy of launching the repertory theatre in its community.

We indicated earlier that one of the primary goals of marketing is efficiency of communication. The aim is first to isolate the prime potential and then to determine the cheapest way of reaching it. Daily newspapers are *mass* media. They reach about everyone within a community. In our case, the combined circulation of the Minneapolis *Star and Tribune* and the St. Paul *Pioneer Press and Dispatch* offer almost saturation coverage of homes in the theatre's Group I, or primary potential area. They also reach well into the rest of Minnesota, parts of Iowa, western Wisconsin, and the Dakotas. Most newspapers, however, are not selective media.

Our prime prospects had been defined as the Yeses and the Maybes, which represented, at most, one fifth of the population. The Noes, we said, were oblivious to message dealing with the theatre and arts. It would be extremely difficult to get the Noes to read advertising about the theatre; if they did, it would be even more difficult to convince them through the printed word that the theatre could be something of importance to them. It is accepted in advertising circles that people do not regularly read ads about products for which they recognize no need. The Noes simply do not believe that they are in the market for the Tyrone Guthrie Theatre. If this is so (and, rightly or wrongly, we decided to accept the premise) then 80 percent of the advertising dollars spent in daily newspapers are wasted. They are not efficient enough to be the primary media.

Critics of our stand on advertising have pointed out that the Sunday *New York Times* (with a 1966 circulation of 1,337,277) is the primary medium for Broadway theatre advertising. Theatrical ads placed there work remarkably well. Isn't it the same situation? It is not the same situation at all. Within the area of primary potential for Broadway theatre the *Times* is a highly selective medium—it does not reach anywhere near the percentage of No households the Minneapolis *Star and Tribune* does, for the people who buy and read the *Times* are primarily Yeses and Maybes. Thus, for Broadway theatre advertising, the *Times* is an efficient buy.

Daily newspapers as a primary medium could be justified if strategy called for a major attempt to persuade not only the Yeses and Maybes but *also* the Noes, that a particular theatre's productions would make everybody happier. Advertising, then, would have to try to convince the Noes to spend their dollars on a specific theatre rather than on some other form of entertainment. If it could be done, it would take a budget as large or larger than the theatre's production budget.

We came to the conclusion that the role of printed communication, including newspaper advertising, was primarily to inform and remind the Yeses and the more susceptible Maybes of the theatre's activities. If the Yeses and Maybes could be isolated accurately, direct mail would be the most efficient way to reach them. But since people cannot easily be identified as to their interest in theatre, some newspaper advertising was necessary to make certain we communicated information and reminders to all those people who were predisposed to attend the Guthrie Theatre. The more reluctant souls, we decided, could only be persuaded in person-to-person contact.

Because of the nature of rolling repertory, it was necessary to run a small ad every day listing the plays to be performed that day and the next. On Sundays we listed the entire week's schedule, similar to the list presented at the beginning of this chapter. The ads were as small as possible to keep expenses down. Aside from these listings, our newspaper advertising was confined almost entirely to medium-sized ads announcing the season-ticket sale, the opening of single-ticket sales, and reminders when each season was about to close. On one or two occasions ads were run quoting from particularly favorable reviews. Other more selective publications were occasionally used, such as suburban newspapers in areas of high potential, and the *Twin Citian* magazine.

In our strategy, newspaper advertising was primarily a public service for those who intended to come, or had been thinking of coming, to the Tyrone Guthrie Theatre. We did not believe then nor do we now that newspaper advertising can sell people on attending classical theatre unless they are inclined to do so in the first place.

From the beginning, the Minnesota Theatre Company employed the services of an advertising agency—the Minneapolis office of BBD&O—not because the theatre intended to do large amounts of advertising, but to get the services of their highly skilled personnel in other areas. Generally, the theatre's public relations staff prepared copy, but the ads were laid out by Bob Englund, BBD&O art director, who also did all the graphic design and layout for other theatre materials. The agency placed space and radio time with the media, handled the billing, and received the standard fifteen percent commission from the media. Radio production assistance was also received from BBD&O, and the agency's research department directed the 1963 audience-analysis study and provided valuable marketing advice in other projects. But the agency's most dramatic help was in the technical assistance it provided on printing production. From the beginning, Dick Arrenholz, an exceptionally imaginative and knowledgeable printing expert, accepted bids and bought all the printing for the theatre. Naturally we were interested in any economies possible without sacrificing quality. During four years of working with Arrenholz, we were able to evolve a system of "gang printing" which resulted in rather substantial cost savings. Perhaps more properly we should say that this system resulted in a substantial increase in the amount of printed material we were able to acquire without corollary increase in costs. An explanation of the concept may be helpful.

Gang printing means the "ganging up" of several different printed pieces on the same sheet of press paper. Paper itself is one of the major costs in printing. It is made by the mills in various standard sheet sizes. If a printed piece is not carefully designed to fill completely (by itself or in multiples) a standard sheet of paper, one pays for the wasted paper. But, because of graphics and sometimes practicality of size, it is not always possible to design a printed piece to fill precisely a press sheet. The resulting wastes can amount to substantial sums of money. Another major cost in printing is "make-ready"—putting plates on a press, registering them, and generally getting the press ready to roll. If a dozen pieces are printed at a dozen different times on a dozen different presses, you pay a dozen make-ready charges. If all 12 pieces are printed on one sheet of paper, on one press, at one time, then there is but one make-ready charge. This charge will not be one-twelfth that required in the former case, but it will represent a substantial saving.

From the point of view of economics, the ideal would be to print all pieces of promotional material at one time, designed in such a way as to make use of every square inch of a standard paper cut. Although we later learned that this ideal is unattainable, we began to explore its possibilities after the 1964 season. At the beginning of each year's promotion, the theatre needed close to 500,000 season-ticket brochures as well as single-ticket brochures, ticket envelopes, group sales flyers, and other printing. In addition, we wanted a number of other printed pieces which we could not afford. Another minor problem was some inconsistency in the appearance of previous materials. For example, in 1964 our color scheme had been black, purple, and green. Yet some of the pieces had been printed only in purple to save the expense of adding another color. Early in the planning for the 1965 season we began exploring a new direction with Arrenholz. We took the biggest standard size sheet of paper that could be put through the biggest available four-color press, a whopping 59 × 77 inches. We designed the season-ticket and single-ticket brochures just as we wanted them and laid them out on the press sheet, putting each brochure on the sheet several times to get proper quantity. We then looked at the space which was unused to see if we could use it after all. Bob Englund began designing other printed material to fit the blank spaces around the edges, fitting them together like a jigsaw puzzle. When we were finished, we had used every square inch of paper—and had included at least five valuable printed pieces we previously had not been able to afford plus the ticket envelopes for the box office. We had a total of 14 different printed pieces, all in four colors and all for about the cost of the previous season's two brochures.

Gang printing on this scale is not practical for every theatre or artistic institution because it demands that a number of items be ready to print at the same time. In many situations this is impossible. But even on a smaller scale it can result in increased productivity for printing dollars. In 1966, at the Trinity Square Playhouse in Providence, Rhode Island, substantial savings were made simply by including the season-ticket brochure, a single-ticket flyer, and the ticket envelopes on the same run. The Long Wharf Theatre in New Haven, Connecticut, used this technique the same year and considerably increased their number of printed pieces.

There are definite economies that come from using the good counsel of experts in print production, and there is much expert help and advice in other fields to be found within the staff of a top advertising agency. In almost every community of any size, there are competent advertising agencies with people who are talented and experienced in diverse fields, people whom an artistic institution cannot afford to hire outright. These fields include copywriting, layout and design, print and broadcast production, research, and efficient buying and placement of advertising time and space. An arts institution may need all of these services or only a few, and an agency will charge fees accordingly. Frequently, an agency can be persuaded to work for a non-profit community institution on a public-service basis, taking standard commissions on advertising purchased, and charging only minimum service fees. The Minneapolis Office of BBD&O handled the Minnesota Theatre Company in this way, charging minimum fees for the time of art and research personnel, taking standard commissions, and making no charges for the handling of print production. The theatre's association with BBD&O was a pleasant and invaluable one.

Chapter 27

Group Sales

The applause died away, the houselights came up, and the audience for an October Saturday matinee performance of The Caucasian Chalk Circle *began to leave the Guthrie Theatre. One group of 38 men and women stayed behind in their seats and soon house manager Archie Sarazin was greeting them.*

"While we're waiting for Lee Richardson to get out of costume, I'll tell you a little bit about the theatre building," Sarazin explained. "Then Lee will talk to you about the play, answer your questions and we'll take you on a tour backstage."

The group was comprised of Rotarians and their wives from a small Minnesota town about 50 miles distant. About one-third of their number had attended the Guthrie Theatre at some time in the first three seasons; now they had decided to rent a bus and come as a group. Two weeks before, Morison had spoken to them in their home town and shown the film, "Miracle in Minnesota." He had given the "Why Bother with Theatre?" speech, followed with background on Brecht and the play.

In the theatre, Richardson—one of the most cooperative and charming of the company—was soon before the group beginning a question-and-answer ses-

*sion which was to last nearly 30 minutes. Finally he
asked for one more question. A short, stocky man
raised his hand. "Could you tell us what plays you'll
be doing next year?" he asked. "We want to start making plans."*

From the beginning we had looked upon the sale of blocks of
tickets to groups as a means, rather than an end in itself—a
way to develop permanent audience rather than just a method
of filling seats. But it took us several years to evolve the concept
of trying to sell the particular package which included a
speaker several weeks before the performance, the film "Miracle in Minnesota," the performance itself, and a discussion
session after the performance, followed by a backstage tour.

The Morison Report had included group sales as a tool for
the development of audience in the Group I area of prime potential. It had called for efforts with three types of groups—
business firms, fund-raising groups, and social groups. It had
recommended that a men's volunteer organization called The
Producers be created primarily to handle sale of blocks of tickets to business firms for customers and employees. Fund-
raising and social groups were to be contacted by direct mail
and through the efforts of The Stagehands and speakers from
the staff. No provisions were made for the hiring of a staff person to handle group sales, which may in part explain why, during four years, we failed to develop a concentrated, well-
organized group-sales effort. The Producers, also, were never
formed while we were with the theatre. By 1966, however, we
had begun to put more time into such efforts and, more importantly, we had evolved what we felt was a satisfactory approach to group sales.

Our reticence in the beginning was due to several factors.
In the first year the season ran from May 7 to September 20.
During this time of the year most organized groups are inactive
and not likely to plan major theatre-going events. We felt, for
that first season at least, energy could be better applied in other
directions. A second factor deterrent to a major group-sales
drive was that the period most advantageous for such a push
coincided with the season-ticket drive. Groups which are most

susceptible to attending the theatre in a body are usually filled with good season-ticket prospects. Here was a conflict: On more than one occasion a Stagehand trying to sell a season ticket was faced with the answer: "I'm going to see *Saint Joan* with my church group, so I'll just buy single tickets for the other shows." Conversely, we met resistance from groups on the grounds that many of their members already had season tickets. We chose to concentrate on season tickets and to read-just our thinking to group sales as a tool for developing audi-ence from the Maybes alone. Later, when the theatre extended its seasons into late October and November, there was more opportunity open to work on group sales.

But there was something else which made us hang back from all-out efforts in group sales early in the game; it was a growing, uneasy feeling that simply selling a group of people who hadn't been to the theatre before on the basis of a discount somehow was *not* the best way to develop a solid, loyal audi-ence. Originally, everyone on the staff had more or less ac-cepted the idea that the main job was simply to get a person into the theatre once and he would become a fan. This may be true with the Yeses and upper echelon of the Maybes, but we are now firmly convinced that more specialized effort is neces-sary with the vast majority of the Maybes and with all of the Noes. Serious theatre demands a great deal of the theatre-goer. Douglas Campbell puts it simply: "It's like love; you have to work at it." But, like love, it has great rewards if one is prepared to cope with the encounter. People conditioned by entertain-ment that is no more demanding than TV or musical comedy are not going to find *Henry V, The Cherry Orchard,* or *The Way of the World* immediately to their liking. They must be pre-pared for what it is they are buying. We have seen too many individuals and groups come to the Guthrie Theatre for the first time not knowing quite what to expect and unprepared for the mental effort. If these people do not enjoy their experience— and many do not—they go away determined not to come back. Worse, they spread the word to their friends. We do not believe this needs to happen, especially if audience development is looked upon as an educational process rather than simply sell-ing. The worst mistake a theatre can make is to sell a group on attending for the first time under the pretense that they are going to see something akin to The Ice Follies.

As we came to understand this, we began to develop the concept of selling the adult education package, and we were able to step up our group-sales efforts without feeling uneasy. In both 1965 and 1966 we printed special group-sales brochures and did extensive mailings. In the fourth season we even had a part-time staff member working on mailings and follow-up. However, we never did push for group sales on the scale that could and should have been done under the education concept. Consequently, there was a small, but gratifying, growth in group sales during the last two seasons. Particularly noticeable was the enthusiasm developed by groups which accepted the entire packages of speaker, film, performance, discussion, and tour.

If we had not left the Minnesota Theatre Company to pursue other plans, we would have extended our efforts in this area and probably tried to create a three-year plan aimed specifically at group sales. Under such a plan, a group would attend at least one play in each of three seasons. The plays would be chosen with an upward trend in sophistication. Working closely with the local public libraries, an expanded program of lectures, audiovisual presentations, and discussions would go in the same direction. Such a program would be ambitious but one with great potential results, for it would help to create a loyal and involved audience rather than merely to sell seats.

Part Eight

Season Tickets

Attracting an audience for a single production is like picking blackberries off a hedge. It takes a lot of leg work, and a long reach, and it is a thorny business at best. In the end, depending on the weather and the changing winds of popular taste, the result may be either feast or famine. But developing an audience for a theatre, for a season, for a succession of seasons—that's gardening.

LEE MITCHELL
Director
Northwestern University Theatre

Chapter 28

Origins of a Philosophy

A dozen people perched on desk tops in the postwar modern house that served as administrative offices for the Minnesota Theatre Company, enthralled by their Sunday morning speaker. It was late fall of 1962 and a half-dozen women volunteers and the theatre's administrative staff had gathered for their first planning meeting for the 1963 season-ticket drive.

The man who had so captured their attention that crisp day was Danny Newman, publicity director for the Chicago Lyric Opera and consultant for the Ford Foundation on season subscription sales. With fiery dedicated enthusiasm he was outlining his recommendations. "Remember," he said, "a single-ticket buyer is your worst enemy. No amount of effort is too much to find that rare and beloved needle in a haystack—the season subscriber."

Newman's advice was worth listening to. In the past decade he had kept the Lyric Opera running at better than 95 percent of capacity and already in his role as a consultant he had produced increases of 300 percent and better in subscriptions for other theatres. Now he was explaining his methods—massive mailings, follow-up mailings, telephone renewal cam-

*paigns, coffee parties—every kind of personal effort
that could be made.*

*He completed his detailed description of tech-
niques and wound up with one final burst of enthusiasm. "Cast your bread upon the waters," he said, "and
it shall come back very much buttered."*

The season subscription "bread" which American resident professional theatre companies have been "casting upon the
waters" under Danny Newman's direction during the past half-
dozen years had indeed been coming back "very much buttered." Today's records show subscription increases for some
theatres as high as 800 percent and touches of the Newman
sales philosophy can be seen in theatre brochures from Seattle
to Baltimore. (The similarity in printed material among resident professional theatres has led at least one wag to refer to
the group as "the Howard Johnson's of the theatre world.")
Though his track record is overwhelming, in many cases the
theatres involved had never before utilized professional help in
preparing material or organizing a drive. The remarkable
increases stem as much from the application of his highly
professional guidance as to a particular formula of promotion.

The original season-ticket sales strategy for the Minnesota
Theatre Company was based on Newman's ideas, and his
counsel and advice were sought in subsequent drives. Though
Newman can scarcely be credited with originating the season
ticket, he can certainly be called the world's most vocal expo-
nent of its worth and the most imaginative promoter of its sales
potential. The season ticket is a promotion package which
offers benefits to both the theatre and the subscriber. Each
gives and receives something in return, theoretically of equal
value, as in the sale of any commodity.

In their simplest form, the benefits of a season ticket purchase to the theatre or other performing arts institution and to
the subscriber can be seen in the table at the top of page
169.

The Theatre Gets	The Subscriber Gets
1. Preopening commitment from the subscriber to attend every production regardless of what the critics say.	1. Ticket priority and assurance of the best seats for each production no matter what the single-ticket response turns out to be.
2. Advance funds to assure that each production can be financed.	2. Discounts—a lower price for each ticket purchased as a series than if purchased individually.
	3. Extra benefits in the form of special social and/or educational benefits available only to subscribers.

The ideal, to Newman, is a total sellout to season-ticket buyers. *Ticket priority* then becomes the strongest selling point and discounts and extra benefits can be minimized. Season tickets can be sold most effectively if the overwhelming reason to purchase them is the fact that you cannot otherwise get in.

The way to this ideal, according to Newman, is a highly refined technique of direct mail and personal contact. The sales appeal is two-pronged: (1) emphasis on discounts (eight plays for the price of six, more than one play free) and (2) a rather frank snob appeal ("Join the theatre-going elite." "Develop theatre taste and discernment." "Enjoy a new dimension of consistency and dignity in your theatre-going.")

The methods Newman expounds are sound:

Use a big, colorful, exciting brochure emphasizing the proper appeals.

Use direct mail, but be selective. Use every mailing list you can get your hands on that includes the *type* of people who are most apt to respond to your appeal.

Don't worry about duplication. The more brochures received by any one person the better.

Send a second and, if necessary, a third brochure or mailing to overcome inertia.

Use women's volunteer organizations to hunt for the needles in the haystack through the personal contact of neighborhood coffee parties.

Use every method possible including telephone campaigns to sell your best potential—previous subscribers.

The Minnesota Theatre Company owes an enormous debt to Newman. The recommendations of the Morison Report on season tickets were based primarily on Newman's ideas, and he deserves a great deal of credit for the excellent results. Newman has said rather adamantly that the decline and fall of the theatre's season-ticket sales can be attributed to our failure to carry out completely his precepts, particularly in the matter of brochure design and copy. This may well be true.

But let us recount our adventures in season-ticket land during four years and then set forth the questions that are raised in our minds about the total validity of the traditional season-ticket approach from the points of view of artistic aspiration as well as of the general health of theatre in this country.

Chapter 29

The Four Campaigns

It was the severest day of January, 1963. By mid-afternoon Sunday, the twenty-first, the temperature had managed to push up to seven degrees below zero. A vicious 25-mile-per-hour wind drove the cold through the boards and flapping plastic that covered the openings to the unfinished Tyrone Guthrie Theatre. In the auditorium the public relations staff scurried about making final preparations for the first event ever held in the theatre: The kickoff meeting for the first season-ticket drive.

A half hour before the scheduled start of proceedings, the participants began to appear, well-bundled and shivering. Peter Zeisler had flown in from New York along with two members of the company, Rita Gam and Claude Woolman. Dave Moore, popular WCCO-TV newscaster, came to do his job as master-of-ceremonies. Oliver Rea soon arrived with Robert Preston. By 15 minutes before starting time only a dozen or so volunteers had struggled in and were stamping their feet vigorously in the lobby; the participants were hustled into backstage areas while the nervous public relations staff went to look, hopefully, for more audience.

At five minutes to the hour, they began to come.

There was a near traffic jam in the streets as cars stopped as close to the door as possible. Other volunteers were fighting the gale on foot from parking lots blocks away. By the time Moore started the program, Preston could look out from one of the entrance tunnels and say, "It's an incredible turnout!" There were almost 800 men and women sitting on the cold concrete and perched on the scaffolding, ready to hear about the drive and willing to sell season tickets.

From the beginning, The Stagehands were looked upon as the key sales force for the Minnesota Theatre Company. Consequently, the Public Relations Department decided to utilize them as any business would utilize its sales force. We tried to give them the benefits of the best possible sales tools and complete cooperation and help from the staff; and we hoped to stir up their enthusiasm with informational sales meetings. Their primary method of selling was to be through neighborhood coffee parties.

This phase of the season-ticket strategy was to remain constant over four seasons, as were several other parts of the first-year plan. The basic promotional medium after the personal contact had been provided by The Stagehands was a massive brochure mailing. Each year the theatre used its own mailing list, which totaled 50,000 by the end of 1966, *plus* the Dayton's department store charge-account list, which numbers in excess of 400,000. Not all persons on Dayton's list could be considered prime season-ticket potential because many lived outside the theatre's 100-mile radius of prime potential and not all were theatre devotees. But they were excellent single-ticket potential. The season-ticket brochure was considered a way of getting basic information about the season into their hands. Advertising for each season-ticket drive was limited primarily to one major ad in the Minneapolis and St. Paul Sunday newspapers. These ads were timed to coincide with the kickoff meeting.

One problem stayed with us over the four years. Because of the complexity of picking dates for the performances the buyer wanted to see, it was difficult to devise a technique by which the volunteers could actually close a sale on the spot. Before a neighbor or friend could fill out the order blank and write a check, she almost always had to spend an evening at home with her husband working out their schedule. The theatre undoubtedly lost many season-ticket sales because of this.

Although the basic components of strategy remained the same for all four campaigns, we did vary techniques and procedures and it may be helpful to review briefly each campaign and the results. As already noted, the first season-ticket drive opened January 21, 1963, and lasted until the theatre opened on May 7, three and one-half months later. The theatre had not yet presented a performance at the time of the drive, so this was a period of anticipation and excitement. The first drive generated its own momentum. The public *wanted* to hear about the theatre and plays; popular curiosity had been stimulated by the publicity which had accompanied the building-fund drive.

The Stagehands (not yet a *formal* organization) had no trouble recruiting 1,400 volunteer workers to carry the work and the literature into the community. Their primary sales tools were the brochure (a six-page, 8½" × 11" folder in red and black) and the 12" long-playing record telling the story of the theatre (see Chapter 20). Their technique was to give coffee parties by the hundreds, drawing upon the theatre staff and a hastily organized volunteer bureau of 30 Junior Leaguers as speakers.

The brochure was mailed first to the list of building-fund contributors, then several weeks later (about the time of the kickoff meeting) to the Dayton's list. Ticket prices that first season ranged from $1.50 to $5, with 10 percent discount on a season ticket. The top season-ticket price was $18.00; the lowest was $4.40. There was no follow-up mailing and no major advertising after the initial newspaper ads had appeared. But publicity came abundantly all through the drive, and volunteer enthusiasm increased as the opening neared. The result of this drive was the sale of 21,295 season tickets, the largest total ever achieved by a theatre. This record was held until the Repertory Company of New York's Lincoln Center launched its first season. The Guthrie Theatre exceeded its own goal of 15,000 season tickets by almost 50 percent and it looked as if the answer had been found to season-ticket promotion.

The success of the first drive had given us no reason to believe we should change our basic promotion plan. In fact, public enthusiasm for the theatre led us to believe that we might be able to increase the total number of season tickets, possibly reaching 30,000. The Stagehands—by this time a formal organization—recruited volunteers for the second season's drive, though the total number of volunteers never again reached the 1,400 of the first year. The speakers' bureau was also in existence as a part of the volunteer group by this time, and the business and professional women's division of The Stagehands had been organized after the audience study showed a weakness in attendance by working girls. But the pattern of the campaign itself was the same, lasting for about three months, and using the coffee party as the key technique but with a bigger and better corps of speakers. The primary sales tools were a brochure and the newly completed film, "Miracle in Minnesota," which was premiered for the volunteers at the kickoff meeting. We had tried to improve the brochure by including more information in a more convenient, usable form. The result was a 16-page booklet, 4" by 8", and printed in the controversial purple and green colors. The price scale for the second season was changed to $5, $3.50 and $2.00, with the $2 ticket sold to any *student* for $1.50. The season-ticket discount remained at 10 percent so that top price was still $18.00 for the four plays, although the lowest price had been raised to $7.20.

The brochure was mailed several weeks in advance to subscribers of the first year, and, later, to the Dayton's list. The drive went well at the beginning, with enthusiasm high, more speaking engagements than ever, and more members of the company and staff making more appearances. There were bigger coffee parties than the first year. On one occasion a suburban couple held an evening open house for the entire neighborhood. Members of the staff and company attended, and the film was shown continuously in the basement. At final count some 250 people had attended.

But toward the end of the second month, orders began to slacken. It seemed apparent that we would not have much of an increase in season tickets, if any, over the previous year. We tried to rekindle enthusiasm and also ran a series of radio spots reminding people that the drive was coming to an end. On opening night in May, 1964, the total stood at 19,483, a drop of 1,812 from the first season.

As we began to evaluate the 1964 campaign, several factors contributing to the decrease began to come to light. For one thing, the volunteers' enthusiasm had lagged toward the end of the second month. The Stagehands told us they thought a three-to-four-month drive was too long—it demanded too much on the part of volunteers and their efforts could not be sustained. An analysis of season-ticket sales by postal zones showed some weakness in areas where the theatre should have done better. We compared it with the home addresses of Stagehand volunteers and discovered that usually where the theatre was weak in volunteers, it was weak in sales. Finally, it became evident from talking with subscribers and from box-office activity that the date-picking problem was a very decided detriment to season-ticket sales. People were having to exchange tickets too many times. We set about trying to solve the problems for 1965.

It was in planning for the third season-ticket drive that the theatre administration first considered using coupons, which people could exchange for tickets, rather than requiring subscribers to pick all dates for tickets in advance. However, with the decision made against coupons, we turned to the problem of trying to sell more season tickets under the same circumstances. We still saw no reason to change our basic tactics, but decided to make some adjustments in them and to try to increase what we had already been doing. We decided to expend more effort in the drive and to shoot for a goal of 30,000 season subscribers.

We began by reorganizing the volunteer organization geographically on an area, district, and block basis to improve coverage in weaker areas. The drive was shortened to two months and the kickoff meeting was limited to area chairmen and district captains, with meetings in the eight districts scheduled twice during the drive. The Stagehands were only partially successful in creating an organization as complete as we would have liked. And we reckoned without Minnesota's March weather. Three consecutive blizzards in ten days effectively snowed-under our plans for the first series of district meetings.

With the mailing list now on electronic tape, it was easy to print out lists of the best prospects (former season- and single-ticket buyers) by postal zones. These lists were arranged by blocks and distributed to block workers who were instructed to contact each person on the lists personally, through a coffee party, a telephone call, or a personal visit.

The plan also called for a basic booklet to be mailed to the same big list, plus a second, follow-up brochure to be mailed to some 80,000 Twin Cities residents, plus a telephone campaign to former subscribers who had not yet renewed two-thirds of the way through the campaign. We were attempting to follow Danny Newman's advice more closely.

We were generally happy with the 4″ × 8″ booklet form of the 1964 brochure, though Newman said it was too small and too restrained. We followed the same format, reducing it to 12 pages to save money for additional follow-up programs. The theatre, however, was in its "conservative-graphics" period and Newman referred to it as "looking like a bank's annual report."

Besides the brochure, the basic sales tool was again the film, "Miracle in Minnesota," since it had shown no signs of wearing out its welcome. We rented three continuous-feed projectors with small self-contained screens to make it easier for the volunteers to handle.

The prices and the discount of 1965 remained the same, with the difference that the theatre was doing five plays—the fifth a revival of *The Miser* from the first season—but the fifth was optional on the season ticket. The total price for four plays was the same as in 1964.

In attempts to counter the date-picking problem, we printed the humorous "date-picker" as well as mail-order exchange blanks which the volunteers were instructed to emphasize. We were off and running.

We didn't have to wait until the half-way point to realize that we weren't going to reach our 30,000 goal. The follow-up brochure produced disappointing results. The same was true of the telephone campaign which had been carried on partly by The Stagehand volunteers and partly by a professional telephone-soliciting service. (We learned it was less expensive and troublesome to use professionals, but that this was no substitute for the enthusiasm of volunteers.) When it became evident that the theatre would fall far short of its goal, we added ammunition. A saturation campaign of radio spots was instituted for a brief period, and a postcard resembling a Western Union telegram was sent to people who had not renewed.

Despite such efforts, we sold only 16,614 season tickets, 2,936 fewer than in 1964 and a loss of 22 percent from the initial 1963 campaign. Reasons for the continuing decline were difficult to analyze. From the telephone campaign we learned, in probing for reasons why a subscriber was not renewing, that the date-picking problem was creating even greater resistance than we had thought, and that the theatre's choice of plays for the repertory was having a decided influence. In assessing the campaign with The Stagehands, they said that the 1965 drive had been too organized. The volunteers felt the demands upon them were so great that they just gave up. Once again we set out to try to remedy the situation.

The first financial deficit to the company occurred during the 1965 season, and the board of directors of the Minnesota Theatre Company decided to raise prices for 1966 to $5.50, $3.75, and $2.50, with the lowest priced ticket for students at $1.50. This, together with the fact that there were to be five new plays in the repertoire, substantially increased the total package price of a season ticket. However, because season-ticket buyers were filling Friday- and Saturday-night houses and forcing the theatre to turn down single-ticket buyers from out of town who could only come on weekends, it was decided to increase the discount to 20 percent for every performance except Friday and Saturday nights. This meant that the top price for a season ticket was $24.75 on Fridays and Saturdays, and $22.00 for the rest of the performances. The lowest price for Fridays and Saturdays was $11.25 and for other performances $10.00. Still a bargain, but substantially greater than the $5.40 low of the first season. Partially to help solve the prob-

lems of date-picking, the "Twin Bill" was instituted, using coupons for the second half of the season.

In addition to increasing discounts, we tried to "sweeten
the pot" by adding extra benefits. Each 1966 subscriber was
given a complimentary copy of the guide to the season, "Setting
the Stage." Five special, "subscriber only" performances, with
symposiums following the play were offered. It was then that
we instituted "Green Room," the bimonthly newsletter published for subscribers.

We planned a shorter, six-week campaign using considerably more visual materials—more posters and Scotchlite
bumper stickers—and a more concentrated effort. We abandoned the booklet form for the brochure and used a slightly
larger—5 × 9 inch, eight-page, fold-out brochure in order
to try for the bigger display impact which Newman thought
necessary. It was mailed to the same large list. Previous subscribers, however, received the brochure, a letter from Rea and
Zeisler, and their copy of "Setting the Stage" neatly packaged in
a transparent plastic envelope. In addition to the brochure, the
basic selling tool was a 12 inch long-playing recording of Dr.
Ballet's lecture on the plays, together with a jazz piece based on
the trumpet fanfare. This record was played at coffee parties. A
follow-up brochure and a telephone campaign were also used.

In an attempt to measure the result of The Stagehands'
work, and to provide an additional technique for closing the
sale, 30,000 self-addressed, postage-paid envelopes were sup-
plied for prospects to use in sending in their orders. Thus, the
stage was set for a more intensive and expansive campaign
offering greater discounts and extra benefits to potential subscribers in the hope of reversing the downward trend of season-
ticket sales in the face of increased subscription prices. The
cost of the campaign was almost half again as much as in previous years.

The campaign got off to a good start. The Stagehands did
a magnificent job of blanketing the town in one weekend with
Op art display material. Radio and TV public service time was
greatly increased through the efforts of newly arrived staff
member Rob Blake, and because of the free distribution of musical director Herb Pilhofer's jazz version of the fanfare. Yet

the results were nowhere near what had been hoped for considering the innovations and the increased amounts of time, effort, and money put into the drive. The postage-paid envelopes proved almost a total failure, with only 200 returned out of the entire 30,000. Similarly, the telephone campaign produced little in the way of renewals. The second mailing, with the follow-up brochure proved even less successful than the previous year's. The total season tickets sold—and this total must be considered in the face of increased total price, also in light of the bigger discounts and the cost of added extra benefits—came to 15,928. Clearly, the time had come for a penetrating look at the traditional season-ticket philosophy and method of sales.

Chapter 30

Some Questions

The results of the 1966 season-ticket drive were in—
Brad Morison, Kay Fliehr, and Rob Blake contem-
plated each other over the luncheon table. More
money, more time, more effort had gone into this
fourth subscription drive than into any previous one.

Blake tried to break the gloom. "All right, do we
really know how much of a selling point a discount
is?" he asked. "Do people really buy a season ticket
because of the money they save?" The other two
shrugged silently. "Let's take a wild example," said
Blake, pushing on. "Suppose we increased our discount
50 percent next season. Six plays for the price of three!
Would we or wouldn't we substantially increase our
sale of season tickets?"

Morison's pencil began to scratch figures on the
back of an old envelope. "If we went to a 50 percent
discount next year, and we kept all 15,928 subscribers
from this year, we'd have to get 81,176 brand new
subscribers before we brought an extra penny of rev-
enue into the till."

The mathematics of season tickets are frighteningly complex
and someday will undoubtedly be left to the infinite wisdom of
a computer. In the meantime it can be both illuminating and

challenging to sharpen the old pencil and indulge in some rough cost analysis and speculative mathematics. Our glum luncheon of July, 1966, led to no solutions, but it did bring about an analysis of *cost per dollar of season-ticket income* so that further speculation could be based on *fact* rather than on *previous* speculation.

Laid out side by side, the facts of the first four seasons are presented in the accompanying table.

A Four-Year Comparison of Minnesota Theatre Company Season-Ticket Sales

	1963	1964	1965	1966
Plays in season ticket	4	4	4 [a]	5
Percent discount	10	10	10	10–20 [b]
Top price for season ticket	$18.00	$18.00	$18.00– $22.50 [a]	$22.00– $24.75 [b]
Length of season (weeks)	20	24	28	28
Percent of capacity played	84.2	82.5	78	66.8
Total attendance	183,931	214,630	239,833	214,172
Season tickets sold	21,295	19,483	16,614	15,928
Season ticket income	$273,060	$253,380	$216,704	$249,317
Cost of season ticket drive	$40,437	$38,556	$38,355	$58,654
Cost per season ticket	$1.74	$1.98	$2.31	$3.68
Cost per dollar of season-ticket income	$.148	$.152	$.177	$.235
Estimated cost per dollar of single-ticket income	$.115	$.116	$.131	$.178

[a] An option of a fifth play was offered for the total subscription price of $22.50.

[b] A 10 percent discount was offered for Friday and Saturday nights only, the season ticket amounting to $24.75. Season tickets for all other nights were offered at 20 per cent discount, the subscription totalling $22.00.

The costs of bringing in each dollar of income had been increasing steadily for both season and single tickets, but the promotion costs for single tickets were from four to six cents lower than for subscribers' dollars. There were no figures from other theatres available for comparison, but we were compelled to ask if there was not a point of diminishing returns, a point where extra money might be more effectively spent promoting single tickets than season tickets.

It is misleading, of course, to read any set of figures too literally. For example, after noting casually that a $20,000 increase in promotion expenditure in 1966 produced a *decrease* in season-ticket sales, one might conclude that the less spent on promotion the better. One must also consider the fact that the increased price of tickets and the increased number of plays offered increased the total package price substantially. It is interesting to speculate what would have happened to total sales without that increased expenditure!

One observation which can be safely made from examination of these statistics is that a relatively constant level of season-ticket promotional efforts over the first three seasons—when all circumstances were similar—failed to prevent a 28 percent decline in the number of season tickets sold. Promotion was not the sole key, however. For one thing, the novelty of the grand opening of a new theatre had partly accounted for the initially large sale of season tickets. One might well expect some decline in interest after the first grand success. But the fact that *total attendance* increased rather substantially over three years (see Table 3 in Appendix) makes it doubtful that the decline in subscribers is solely due to the fading novelty of the theatre.

There is a theory that when season-ticket sales are good, single-ticket sales are also excellent. This implies that single sales are dependent upon season sales. There is no real evidence to support such a correlation. In light of present evidence, the only valid conclusion is that, if there are good and exciting reasons for buying season tickets, those reasons also stimulate single-ticket sales. Our own evidence shows that *total* sales can go up substantially even when season sales decline.

From our experience we know, also, that the difficulty of

picking dates months in advance in a system of rolling repertory can discourage a great deal of repeat buying of season tickets.

But for the real reason behind declining season-ticket sales in the face of a constant level of promotional effort, and hopefully with improved techniques, one has only to look at the percentage of total capacity at which the theatre operated during the first four seasons. At no time, except in the final few weeks of each season, was it difficult for a single-ticket buyer to get a seat, even at the last minute. Ticket priority, as a reason for subscribing, was eliminated as a sales incentive. There was no real pressure at the box office, and the season-ticket buyer soon discovered that he did not have to subject himself to the inconvenience of picking dates, and making subsequent exchanges in order to get a seat for a performance. The theatre was asking for a difficult advance commitment from subscribers and giving little in return—a 10 percent discount, no ticket priority, and no extra benefits.

In approaching the 1966 season we were faced with increased ticket prices and a five-play series which increased the total cost of season tickets by about a third. To meet this challenge, discounts were increased slightly, and extra benefits—in the form of the newsletter, "Setting the Stage," and Sunday symposiums—were added. Also the "Twin Bill" for easier date-picking was introduced. Total promotional expenses were increased by about half. The net result was to *maintain* the sale of season tickets at almost the same level as in 1965.

Now some pertinent questions became apparent:

1. All else being equal, would a similar promotional expenditure in 1967 bring in a similar number of subscribers? Had the theatre reached a kind of plateau?

2. If so, is 23.5 cents per dollar of subscription income a justifiable expense with respect to the cost per dollar of single-ticket income?

3. Could promotion costs be reduced without substantially reducing the number of subscribers?

4. Could substantially increased promotion expenditures increase the total number of subscribers?

Take the latter possibility—increasing the total number of

subscribers with increased promotional funds. Ticket priority as a strong selling point has been eliminated. To increase sales we must look to the next possible selling point: an increase in discounts. This calls for some hypothetical and speculative mathematics. The best prospect for a *new* season-ticket sale is a current single-ticket buyer. It is unrealistic to think that one can corner a stranger on the street who has never been in the theatre and sell him a five-play series.

For the sake of such hypothetical mathematics, let us assume the following:

Top ticket price: $5.00

Number of current subscribers at $5.00: 4,000

Revenue realized per season-ticket holder on five-play season: $20.00

Number of plays seen by average single-ticket buyer: 2.2 (actual at the Guthrie Theatre)

Amount of revenue realized from average single-ticket buyer: $12.00

Now let us assume that, in order to try to increase total number of season tickets, we increase the discount from twenty to thirty percent. This increase in discount is designed to convert a single-ticket buyer to a season subscriber. So we need a new set of figures:

Revenue realized per season-ticket holder on five-play season at 30 percent discount: $17.50

Loss of income per season ticket resulting from increased discount for present subscribers: $2.50

Total loss of income 4,000 subscribers at $2.50 each: $10,000

Next we must compute our gain in income from converting one single-ticket buyer to a season-ticket buyer:

Income from purchase of season ticket at 30 percent discount: $17.50

Income from single-ticket buyer attending 2.2 plays at full price: $12.00

Total gain in income from converting single-ticket buyer to season purchase: $5.50

On this basis the number of new subscribers needed to compensate for the $10,000 loss in revenue due to increased discount becomes

$$\frac{\$10,000}{\$5.50} = 1{,}818 \; new \; subscribers$$

Thus we must convert a minimum of 1,818 single-ticket buyers into subscribers just to make up for the money lost by increasing the discounts to subscribers. And this does not take into account the probable increase in sales costs necessary to make the conversion from single to season buyer. *A gain of almost 50 percent in subscribers is necessary in this case just to make up for a 10 percent increase in discount.*

This is not to suggest that an increase of 10 percent *would not* produce a 50 percent increase in sales (though there is little evidence to support that it would); the point is only to suggest that the mathematics of season tickets, discounts, and sales costs is so complex and involved that it can be sheer disaster to toy with a delicate balance in a cavalier manner.

How the Minnesota Theatre Company will cope with the complex mathematics of season tickets and the new problems of an eight-play season in two theatres remains to be seen. But the experience of the first four years leads us to a positive conclusion and several important questions:

It seems evident that the only truly effective, efficient and economical season-ticket program is one which is based upon almost total sellout to season-ticket buyers year after year. Under these circumstances, only minimum discounts and extra benefits *and* minimum promotional expenses are necessary; renewals come easily when there is no other way of getting a ticket to the theatre.

In many theatre situations, total sellout on season tickets will never be possible. If a subscription program based on sellouts to subscribers *is* impossible, the remaining incentive for a person to make advance commitment must be in discounts and extra benefits, both costly to the theatre. Under these circumstances, isn't it possible that the subscriber-at-any-cost philosophy is invalid? Isn't it possible, beyond a certain plateau of subscribers whose renewals are based primarily on loyalty, that the cost per dollar of season-ticket income achieved through discounts and extra benefits will be so far above costs per dollar for single-ticket income that the expenditure will not be justified?

Assuming that it was possible to sell out to season-ticket buyers, is it actually desirable? Despite the guaranteed nucleus that subscribers constitute for the company, does year-after-year sellout to the same people result in artistic stagnation? Does it prevent the accomplishment of one responsibility of a theatre: the introduction of new people to the theatrical experience? Does it perpetuate the "arts-for-the-few" tradition in an age when the arts should be moving from the periphery toward the center of society? Is it possible that the traditional season-ticket concepts are being outdated by the new challenges for the performing arts in an affluent society, and that new creative approaches must be taken to obtain financial and philosophic commitments from audiences?

We don't pretend to know the answers. We only claim the questions are worthy of debate.

Part Nine

Educating Tomorrow's Audience

Only minor attention has been given [by American schools] to cultivating the artistic taste of the large mass of students not engaged in performing organizations.

Rockefeller Panel Report,
The Performing Arts: Problems and Prospects

Chapter 31

High-School Matinees

Barton Emmet sat on a wooden stool in the shadows of a niche in the back of the house just off aisle 8. He was fascinated with what he was seeing and hearing. The third performance of Hamlet for high-school students in the spring of 1963 was over, and actors George Grizzard and Lee Richardson, still in costume, were on stage answering a steady flow of questions from the teenagers.

"Why was the style of the play mixed up? Why didn't Hamlet use a gun instead of a sword when he killed Polonius?" As Grizzard launched into his answer, Emmet puzzled over the difference between the questions that day and those at the previous performance. Yesterday the question-and-answer session had been over quickly. The questions had been more in the vein of "How old are you?" and "Are you married?" And Emmet remembered, yesterday's audience had been much more restless and inattentive during the performance itself. As he looked around the house trying to discover the difference between the two audiences, he was aware of a figure slipping in beside him. It was house manager Archie Sarazin with a message.

"Some of the bus drivers are wondering if you couldn't break this thing up," Sarazin whispered.

"They're supposed to get the kids back to the schools by six P.M."

The high-school matinees of the Minnesota Theatre Company's first season were a fascinating experience for both actors and the company's staff who monitored such performances anxiously. While the actors were enthusiastic about all of the student audiences, it became evident that there were striking differences among them, and an intriguing search for reasons started that first spring and led to some interesting conclusions.

Presenting special matinees for high-school students is not a new idea. The theatres in Stratford, Connecticut, and Stratford, Ontario, had been doing it for years, and many other theatres make special arrangement for high schools today. The program at the Tyrone Guthrie Theatre has been highly successful, and grew from a total of seven performances in 1963 to 26 in 1966, with a total of more than 120,000 students attending during the first four years. For many schools, some as far away as 500 miles, a trip to the Guthrie each spring has become a tradition.

The concept of such special student matinees is ideal for a theatre. Everybody benefits. The students see professional drama at a reduced price. The English teacher often bases a study unit on the play and uses the theatrical experience as a way of putting new excitement into the teaching of dramatic literature. The actors polish their performance before live and highly critical audiences before playing to the adult public. The director can alter and cut on the basis of audience reaction. And the theatre hopes it is building a strong and aware audience for the future. Whether school programs as now presented are effectively accomplishing this end is a question we shall deal with later in this section.

There are many other benefits to the Guthrie Theatre's high-school matinee program. Johnny's excited dinner-table résumé of his experience at the theatre may arouse the interest of Mother and Dad who may themselves become a part of the Guthrie audience. Civic leaders can become aware that the theatre is interested in serving the community on many levels, not just in selling tickets. And when the big yellow school buses from River Falls, Wisconsin, Winnipeg, Manitoba, and Cherokee, Iowa spilled out hordes of hungry teenagers into the stores and restaurants, the business community beamed benevolently upon the Guthrie.

That part of the Morison Report which outlined a plan for student matinees was written by Barton Emmet, based on his experience at the American Shakespeare Festival in Stratford, Connecticut. The program called for special performances in May, June, and September with the whole house set aside for students and all tickets priced at $1.50. Each teacher or other chaperone for every 20 students was to receive a free ticket. Background materials on the play were to be sent to the high-school classes as soon as their ticket reservations were confirmed. The final part of Emmet's recommendation called for the short talk and question-and-answer period at the end of each performance. The plan was carried out as outlined except that the theatre did not schedule high-school performances in September of that first season and, unfortunately, we did not find time or money to prepare background material on the plays for the classes.

In 1962, Emmet presented the plan for student matinees to the State Commissioner of Education and got immediate, enthusiastic response. The Commissioner offered to include an announcement of the theatre's student program with Department of Education mailings. But Emmet refused the offer. He wanted to be able to do a more careful job of selling the teachers on the program as a way to enhance their students' experience in dramatic literature. As he knew from talks with teachers and school officials, there was often resistance from some school superintendents and principals to releasing students from class time for theatre trips. Emmet wanted to work on that problem first.

He began the promotion of the high-school matinees by sending a letter to all school superintendents and high-school principals telling them of the program, asking their cooperation, and advising them that the theatre would be contacting their English teachers directly. This was important strategy. Then, in January, 1963, with the schedule set for five matinees of *Hamlet* and four of *The Miser* in late April and early May, a letter explaining the plan and a ticket-order blank went to all high-school English teachers in the state. Orders were filled on a first-come, first-served basis and more came than could be served. Emmet began to plan for a greatly increased school schedule in 1964.

The number of performances was increased to 27 in the second season, with some scheduled in the fall. Twenty-eight were filled to capacity in 1965, but this number had to be reduced to 26 in 1966 because of rehearsal schedules, although many school groups attended regular Wednesday matinees at the $1.50 student rate.

The differences among the reactions of those first student audiences seemed to have little to do with any differences in where the students came from, or with the socioeconomic differences among the high schools. We began to talk with teachers and students at intermission and to listen carefully to the nature of the questions asked after the performance. One difference soon became evident. The more carefully the teachers had prepared the students, the more attentive, well-disciplined, aware, and perceptive they were in the theatre. When the students came from classes where enthusiastic teachers had taught the play well and given them proper perspective on their coming adventure in living theatre, the audiences were enthusiastic. When the students came primarily from classes where the play had only been touched upon in a pedantic manner and the teacher looked upon the trip only as another chaperoning job, the audiences were more restless, less responsive. Apparently the teacher was a very important element in the student's enjoyment of the theatrical experience. We began to wonder what the theatre could do the following season to encourage and help teachers do a better job of preparing students, both from a literary and a psychological point of view. Perhaps it had been a serious mistake not to find the time and money to prepare the background material which Emmet had recommended be sent to the teachers well in advance of performance.

We decided to seek advice from the most logical source— a teacher. It had come to our attention that Michael Fleming, a young English teacher at Minneapolis' Marshall High School, had done a thorough and imaginative job of preparing his classes to see *Hamlet,* and of using the performance as a classroom tool for further learning. Fleming had chosen *not* to have his classes read the play, but, instead, explored Shakespeare in great detail—his world and his theatre. The class built a model of the Globe Theatre. They did read a few selected portions of the play, but further, they rented the Laurence Olivier film of *Hamlet.* Each student paid 50 cents toward the cost of the film rental since the school had no budget for such materials. After viewing the film, the students discussed the plot, and when they had attended the Minnesota Theatre Company production, they engaged in lively discussions for several weeks about the relative merits of the film vs. the stage media, and the differences in interpretation between the two productions. Fleming had set his classes on fire with enthusiasm for Shakespeare, *Hamlet,* and the Guthrie Theatre.

Fleming's advice was simple: "Prepare material directed at giving the *teacher* background on theatre and the plays, not the students," he said. "Most high-school English teachers are not prepared to teach dramatic literature. They don't have time to prepare themselves, and they don't like to admit that they *need* such preparation. If you don't give them help, they will simply make a perfunctory gesture of preparing their students." This was advice which we were to hear over and over again as the theatre launched a growing program of study guides and educational activities.

Chapter 32

Setting the Stage

The following excerpt appeared in the Foreword to the 1965 school edition of the season study guide, "Setting the Stage":

We received many welcome comments from you about the study kit we prepared last season. After considering these comments carefully, we decided that it would be extremely beneficial to the project for us to seek the advice of people who would use the kits in the future. With this in mind, we appointed an Educational Advisory Council for the theatre and held our first meeting on September 23, 1964. The meeting proved most valuable. Again this season, in consultation with Michael Fleming and Professor Arthur Ballet, we have prepared some background material on the plays. We hope that you will find this study book useful whether or not your classes are able to attend our student performances.

We plan to continue this study book idea for as long as you find it valuable, and encourage you to guide us and the Council in the preparation of future materials.

Sincerely yours,
Oliver Rea   Peter Zeisler
Co-Managing Directors

The study kit referred to by Rea and Zeisler was a rather make-shift affair prepared for the second season when Shakespeare's *Henry V* and Shaw's *Saint Joan* were given for high schools. Michael Fleming, hired as a consultant, prepared about two dozen mimeographed pages of suggestions on methods of teaching Shakespeare's plays and relating them to Shakespeare's England; on the fifteenth century; and on Shaw as a playwright. He also compiled a bibliography, including study aids such as films and recordings. This material, together with four 8½ × 11 inch printed sheets with costume sketches, drawings, and photos of platform stages, was inserted in a purple folder and sent to every teacher who ordered tickets for the 1964 student matinees. The kits were well received and the 27 performances of the two plays in April and May were sold out.

Many high schools took advantage of the historical nature of the plays to study related material in classes other than English. At Our Lady of Peace High School in St. Paul, curriculums for the winter term in history, music, art, and English were built around *Saint Joan, Henry V*, and the fifteenth century generally. Some teachers were using the theatre as a classroom resource far beyond our anticipations, and possibilities began to open up in our minds for study materials that went far beyond the scope of our original intentions.

But as we thought about an expansion of the study kit for 1965, we began to feel a bit uneasy. Even though we were drawing upon the good counsel of Fleming, the theatre was beginning to put itself in the position of an educator. And neither we nor the rest of the theatre staff were qualified for that. We decided to organize a well-balanced committee of educational experts to guide us further. On September 23, 1964, the first meeting of the Minnesota Theatre Company Secondary Education Advisory Council was held. It included the State Commissioner of Education; representatives of the schools of education, theatre and liberal arts at the University of Minnesota; and outstanding speech and English teachers from Minnesota and the four surrounding states. Their assistance and advice during two years was invaluable to the development of the theatre's educational programs.

The purpose of the first meeting was primarily to review the 1964 study kit and make recommendations for the next year. The Council immediately confirmed Fleming's initial observations about teachers. Yes, they said, direct the study materials toward the teacher. There are many outstanding teachers with great knowledge of and enthusiasm for the theater. But they are in the minority. The majority of English teachers are ill-prepared by training or experience to cope with the teaching of dramatic literature in an exciting way. Even if they are inclined toward thorough preparation of a class before attending the theatre, the demands upon their time are such that the amount of research they can do is limited. Approach the study guide as if you were doing the research that the teacher should do to prepare a class well for the performance was the Council's advice. One of the members of the Council later put it more strongly in a letter: "They [English teachers] show an amazing indifference to the performing arts as such, and are reluctant to give way to the theatre if it cuts into their teaching time devoted to literature and composition."

The Council had some other advice about the material for 1965. In addition to background on the plays and playwrights, they suggested we include articles on related areas of history, music, and art. Include pieces on living theatre itself—how to enjoy watching a play, how to read a play. Include interesting stories on how a production is actually put together at the Tyrone Guthrie Theatre. And they suggested the use of more visual materials—costume sketches, pictures of the company in previous roles, photographs of other productions of the plays, and pictures of backstage activity and shops.

The group also pointed out that many of the teachers who were bringing classes to the theatre probably were not those in dire need of help. We were speaking to those who didn't need the advice if we limited distribution of materials only to those who ordered tickets. Perhaps, the Council suggested, a teacher who was reluctant about teaching a play and bringing a class to the theatre would take new courage and plunge in if armed with the study guide. Send it to *all* English teachers, they suggested.

The film, "Miracle in Minnesota," had been widely used by

teachers in preparing classes for their theatrical adventure during the winter and spring of 1964. The Council had one other recommendation—that we find the resources to begin to create a *library* of audio-visual materials on the Guthrie Theatre. We were overwhelmed with good suggestions and advice but obviously could not do everything at once. We began with the background materials for the 1965 season. The plays for the student matinees were Shakespeare's *Richard III* and *The Way of the World* by William Congreve. Under Fleming's direction, and counseled by Dr. Arthur Ballet, a member of the Advisory Council, the study kit became a 24-page, 9 × 12 inch booklet called "Setting the Stage." It contained increased visual material, articles by Fleming on the Restoration period, and how to enjoy a play, an article by the theatre's playwright in residence, James Lineburger, on a production in the making, plus background on the plays and their authors. In line with the Council's recommendation, one copy was distributed free to every English teacher in the state of Minnesota and parts of the surrounding states. "Setting the Stage" was extremely well received and, despite the fact that it was written for teachers, we got orders from many schools for 25 to 50 more copies for distribution to the students. (We charged 50 cents each for additional copies.)

"Setting the Stage" was also taking another direction. During the second season we had received many requests from adults for background information on the plays, and we had given them remaining copies of the material Fleming had prepared for high schools. We discovered that many adult organizations were studying the plays. Some Great Books groups had turned to the season's plays for new study and discussion material. Under the direction of Bob and Maggie Morgan, the Scott-Dakota County Library system held study and discussion sessions. There were increasing calls to the theatre for "anything and everything you have on the plays."

Delighted by the real and genuine adult interest in probing into the theatre more deeply, a second version of "Setting the Stage" was published. This also was a 24-page booklet, but it contained background on all five plays rather than just the two included in the high-school version. Since the material on

Richard III and *The Way of the World* had been written for adults, it could be used in the other edition as well. The adult version of "Setting the Stage" was distributed free through state library departments to nearly 2,500 public libraries in five states and sold at 50 cents per copy to study groups. Our supply of 8,000 was quickly exhausted and comments were enthusiastic.

In the fall of 1965, the Educational Advisory Council met to assess the product and to make suggestions for the following year. They were our "ears" in the educational community. Their report: Good, but it could be better. Reach out for your contributors and get recognized authorities from the area and the rest of the country to write articles. Provide a larger bibliography and delve more deeply into the technical end of production. The Council also reported that more and more teachers were taking small groups of students to some of the plays other than the special high-school performances. Further, students were beginning to go on their own. There was no need for two separate versions of "Setting the Stage," they said. One edition on all five plays could be used for both adult groups and high schools.

We followed their advice. "Setting the Stage" for 1966 was a 32-page booklet with background, written by recognized authorities in their fields, on each of the five plays. Included were pieces by Alrik Gustafson, chairman of the Department of Scandanavian Studies at the University of Minnesota and an internationally recognized Strindberg scholar; Dr. Stanley Weintraub, Professor of English at Pennsylvania State University, editor of *The Shaw Review,* and noted authority on Bernard Shaw; and a reminiscence by Fredric March on the first production of *The Skin of Our Teeth.*

By the time the 1966 edition was being planned, we had also created a Library Advisory Board to counsel us on adult study programs and adult uses of "Setting the Stage." They helped us to increase the size of the bibliography and suggested that adult groups would like to have guidance for discussions of the plays. With the help of the Great Books organization, a section called "Topics for Discussion" was prepared, which included questions pertinent to each play.

This time, 25,000 copies were printed and distributed to libraries and schools. In addition, a copy was given to each season subscriber. The remainder were sold for 50 cents, and the sale had to be cut off in September when our file copies were being threatened. Total cost for the 1966 edition of "Setting the Stage" was approximately $8,000.

In four years, with the help of many good friends and advisors, the theatre had a smoothly functioning high-school matinee program and an evolving program for helping teachers to increase student enjoyment. It also had initiated a publication aimed at helping in that program as well as at helping to increase the interest and knowledgeability among the regular audience. The primary purpose of all this was to maintain and substantially enlarge the total audience of the future.

But as 1966 passed our experience and some new events began to make us wonder whether the students who were passing in and out of the theatre would really come back on their own as adults. We began to question whether high-school matinee programs in their present form were really effective tools in building an audience for the future.

Chapter 33

Does It Work?

The bell clanged in the hallways of a suburban Minneapolis high school signalling the beginning of sixth hour. In a tenth-grade mathematics classroom, the preclass conversation bubbled with even more enthusiasm than usual that May afternoon. Today the subject was theatre; for about one-third of the class had been absent from math the previous day, attending a student matinee of The Skin of Our Teeth *at the Guthrie Theatre with their Enriched English group. Now there were animated descriptions of the performance and the theatre for the benefit of the friends in math class who had missed it.*

Soon the teacher, a man who also served as an assistant football coach, strode into the room and demanded silence and attention in no uncertain terms. "We've got work to do," he said, and then added sardonically, "And all you odd balls who wasted yesterday flitting off to the theatre have got to work twice as hard to make up what you missed on something really *important."*

The task of making confirmed theatre-goers out of teenagers through school performances is beset by many problems, including the active hostility of some teachers, principals, parents and student peers. The happy theory is that the opportunity to bring English classes to performances of theatre will make more effective the teaching of dramatic literature, and that this early exposure to theatre (or any of the arts) will help the student to develop a life-long taste. We have our doubts about the validity of the theory.

William J. Baumol and William G. Bowen, in their book, *Performing Arts: The Economic Dilemma,* say:

> It should be made clear that while the logic of this argument is acceptable enough, it rests also on an allegation of fact which has yet to be tested: The hypothesis that taste for the arts is instilled by early experience. No one seems to have any overpowering evidence that this is so. No one has yet tracked down the children who have attended the New York Philharmonic young people's concerts which were given continuously from 1898 . . . until 1939, or the WPA performances, to see whether they subsequently showed greater interest in the arts than persons coming from otherwise similar backgrounds.

We do not question the premise that early exposure to art *under the right conditions* may instill a life-long interest. Our experience only leads us to question whether the theatre's current programs, which are similar to those in several other theatres, constitute the right conditions. There seem to us to be too many negative pressures operating against the positive influence of a performance to create any distinct and long-lasting favorable impression on the high-school student. We believe that the ultimate effect upon students of attending a performance depends, to a large measure, upon the attitude with which the individual teacher approaches the experience. If a teacher is enthusiastic about living theatre—presents it as one of the many entertaining experiences that are part of life, relates it as a medium to motion pictures and television, and deals with the play as the bone structure for performance—then the conditions would seem to be right. The teacher may then inspire the student to expect entertainment rather than an extension of classroom learning and the student is more likely to enjoy the performance. If this happens, theatre will have been put into a framework of entertainment rather than more academic exercise.

On the other hand, if the teacher looks upon the theatrical performance simply as a way of bringing home more forcefully the traditional academic dissection of plays as dramatic literature, then the student has less chance to look on theatre as an entertaining adventure. He approaches it as "more of the same," except that he gets out of school to do it. The theatre becomes something connected with schoolwork rather than a part of nonacademic life. And if the student's home environment has not included theatre, he will be inclined to categorize it forever as an academic matter to be shucked off quickly along with the rest of school tasks upon graduation. Worse yet, of course, are the conditions created by a teacher who does not prepare the children at all and may, in fact, look upon the whole journey to the theatre as an imposition.

In the Midwest, most high schools which have sent classes to student matinees at the Tyrone Guthrie Theatre have been selective. They sent either the enrichment classes or the high-achieving students, or they have let the teachers themselves decide whether to take their classes. In very few cases has a school sent the entire student body or a whole grade. This has meant that, on the whole, most students attending have been at least reasonably well-prepared because primarily only the most interested teachers and the brightest students have been involved.

On the other hand, in some of the new experiments such as the Government's laboratory theatre program in Providence, Rhode Island, every student in every high school is attending performances. There is nothing particularly wrong with this, except it means that every English teacher in every high school is forced to become involved. The possibility exists that more harm than good can be done by the attitude of ineffectual teachers pushed into participation.

As we became more aware of the influence which teachers have on school programs as audience-development tools, we began to search for some answers. The problem of teachers and effective preparation of students was frequently discussed with the theatre's Educational Advisory Council. "Setting the

Stage" was a first step, but there was agreement that the problem could not be solved merely by waving a study guide under the teacher's nose. The root of the problem lay deeper—probably somewhere back in the schools which educate the teachers. Together with the Council we devised a plan to begin to attack the problem: An annual workshop on the teaching of dramatic literature, to involve educators, teachers, actors, directors, and designers. The purpose: to discuss and exchange new and creative ideas for the teaching of theatre and dramatic literature. A well-qualified teacher-cum-drama student was drafted from The Stagehands' special projects division to contact educators and arrange for meetings between the University, the State Department of Education, and teachers from our Advisory Council. Marjorie D'Aquilla struggled to bring about a starting dialogue, but the project became mired in the swamp of pedagoguese. The scope of such a workshop, and the problems of interdepartmental intrusions that it uncovered, soon convinced us that we were in far over our heads, and the plan died a quiet, unobserved death. The problem is too great for any one organization to tackle. We feel it will take years of adjustment and maneuvering before any progress can be made.

But our experiences in the field do lead us to ask some questions. Does a teenager's experience with the theatre through high schools have any affect upon developing a life-long taste for it? Can this experience have any positive effect without a superbly effective teacher preparing the way? Are the majority of today's teachers equipped to prepare students for the theatrical experience? Is it possible that our theatre had been ahead of itself in trying to develop future audiences by promoting student attendance? Is it possible that theatres should first of all concentrate on teachers? Should theatres perhaps be working on a major informational and educational program for teachers and teachers-to-be through schools of teacher education?

We also were aware of the importance of other students' attitudes. A student who has enjoyed a theatrical performance and says so out loud may find himself the target of snickers from his friends and derisive comments from some teachers, the principal, and possibly even his parents. If enjoyment of theatre is not "in" with a student's general peer group and among adults whom he admires—and if it appears that he will be "out" if he *does* enjoy theatre—then he may file it away as a mistake in order to retain his stamp of social approval.

At the same time that high-school students were being exposed to the Guthrie Theatre in an educational context, it seemed important to us that they also be exposed to it on a social level, away from whatever stigma they attached to the classroom. Perhaps some promotions for teenagers outside of school would help to prove to them that theatre was also a socially acceptable form of entertainment.

We began to ponder what such promotions might be, and came to the realization that we were too far removed from our own teens to have any notion what to do. Again we called on the special projects division of The Stagehands and asked them to form a Teen Advisory Council. Lorrie Lennon and Marcia Hinitz, both former teachers, enthusiastically contacted the counselors and administrative staffs of Twin Cities and suburban high schools. They specifically requested the names of "all-around" students, potential leaders of the student body who were not theatre buffs or looked on as "egg-heads" by their peers. We wanted to counter the forces that tend to make enjoyment of theatre an "out" thing with much of the student body.

What we had at the first meeting in April, 1966 were 49 "swingers," bristling with ideas. We explained our purposes: To encourage students to come to the theatre on their own, not just because the teacher said they must. We spent the rest of the year trying to dig out from under the avalanche of suggestions they gave us.

Did they want a dance in the theatre after a performance? No, that was "square." They'd rather meet with the actors and have cokes . . . "And don't *you* buy the cokes. That puts the wrong emphasis on it. Let the students be like adults and buy their own cokes." Should we try for spot announcements on a certain radio station? No! That station was *out* three months ago. Everybody listens to the other one. Most of our adult ideas would have been sudden death. We were given a stinging lesson on the old adage: If you want to sell a certain group, ask *them* what they want to buy.

With little advance notice, the Teen Advisory Council organized a special Teen Night. They urged their classmates to attend by mimeographing and mailing thousands of personally signed announcements. They then acted as hosts to the 400 teenagers who joined the company after the performance for conversation and cokes—paid for by the students. They volunteered as tour guides, set up a teen speaker's bureau, and asked for, and got, a comprehensive one-day training session with designers, directors, technical, and administrative staff. "If we're going to get people interested in the theatre, we have to know what we're talking about," they said.

In short, the teens "swing." Their exuberant acceptance of tasks and problems was a continual boost to the theatre. There is no end to what they would not or could not do if the council is continued. We are convinced that it was the beginning of a program which can help put theatre in the proper social and entertainment context at the same time that the student matinee program works to relate theatre to history, music, art, literature, and life. Both programs, we feel, are important to developing audiences for the future—for these questions still nag at us: Is an experience with theatre through the high school classroom *enough* to counteract family and peer (and possibly educators') prejudice against it? Will students rebel against the theatre experiences in later life (as they rebel against other academic experiences) if the only place they encounter it is high school? Is high school too late to develop an interest in theatre? Do today's teenagers mature so much faster that their habit patterns are too firmly established by high school for their attitudes to be changed? For the young, shouldn't as much emphasis be placed on the theatre as a social experience as is placed on it as an academic experience?

Part Ten

And in Conclusion

Effective development of the arts . . . becomes, in our
time and country, a matter of developing an audience as
much as it does of training the artist.

The Rockefeller Panel Report,
The Performing Arts: Problems and Prospects.

Chapter 34

Some Opinions

A high-school boy from a middle-class suburb of the Twin Cities was being interviewed by a reporter for the local weekly newspaper. He was one of many students being asked for their reactions to a new enriched-arts lecture course. It was spring, the school year was coming to an end, and the paper was doing a feature on both student and teacher impressions of the experiment. "How did you like it?" asked the reporter. "What was it like to hear all about the arts?"

The boy was silent for a long while, his hand running nervously through his hair. Finally he spoke. "It was like walking down a long, dark corridor with many doors, and having them opened at least a crack. If you don't remember the rooms, at least you remember the hall and know where to go. And you aren't afraid anymore."

This book has been an attempt to recount our experiences in four years of audience-development work for the Minnesota Theatre Company at the Tyrone Guthrie Theatre in Minneapolis. We have tried to present the questions which this experience has brought to our minds. We do not claim to know the answers, but we do have some opinions which we hope will be valuable not only to other theatres but also to all arts institutions.

We firmly believe that the arts, in our time and country, have a new responsibility to "open the doors at least a crack" for the large majority of the population who live behind the Cultural Curtain. It is necessary that we expand our audience, not only to enlarge it but also to make it representative of the total society. The task is not easy or short. But we now believe it to be realistically possible and imperative. Contemporary America is a society unique in the history of civilization. For the first time the majority of a nation's population has been released from the burdens of survival. The great bulk of America's people need no longer expend their entire energy in pursuit of food, clothing, and shelter. They may turn much of their time toward pleasure, conveniences, and comfort and, if they so choose, toward the pursuit of wisdom, beauty, and truth.

With the first emergence of this new freedom, Americans turned their released time and energy toward the consumption and accumulation of material goods. But in the past ten years there is evidence of substantially increased public interest in adult education, religion, travel, the humanities, and the arts. We believe this to be the beginning of a search by Americans for a way to occupy their released energies in a way that is more meaningful and rewarding than cultivated affluence. But because there is no precedent for a society such as ours, and because America is a young nation without long-established traditions, the search is a groping one.

The problems which accompany increased leisure time are not yet fully with us, but they are clearly predictable and their implications are frightening. Dr. Richard Bellman, mathematician for the Rand Corporation has been quoted as predicting that the day is coming when two percent of our population, working in factory and on farm, will be able to produce all the goods and food that the other 98 percent can possibly consume. He believes that this day will arrive no later than 25 years from now, and more likely will arrive in about ten years.[1] An economist has stated: "The United States faces such an explosive

[1] *Quoting Ernest Favemann, "The Emptiness of Too Much Leisure,"* Life *Magazine, February 14, 1964, p. 85.*

increase in leisure time in the next ten years that we may have to keep the unemployed portion of our population under more or less constant sedation." [2] The implication of these two statements represents what may be the greatest challenge of the latter half of the twentieth century.

If those connected with cultural institutions believe that involvement with the arts is a preferable alternative to constant sedation, then it becomes their responsibility to "open the doors at least a crack" for as much of the population as possible. Most people by themselves cannot open the doors. They are in a "long, dark corridor" and they are afraid. The arts must accept the challenge and do everything within their power to open the doors. No person or institution can accept the benefits of membership in society without accepting the responsibilities.

Even if there were not moral and social reasons for attempting to make audiences for the arts more representative of society, there would seem to be other reasons that are just as valid. Baumol and Bowen, in their study of the economic dilemma of the performing arts,[3] present a persuasive case for the fact that the gap between income and expenditure for the arts will continue to increase in coming years. The answer must be increased individual, foundation, and corporate giving and, particularly, increased governmental assistance. August Heckscher, director of the Twentieth Century Fund at the time it sponsored the study, says in his Foreword: "Without wanting to apportion the economic charge, I suggest that the analysis and the figures contained in this report point the way to a considerably larger contribution by government."

If a considerably larger government contribution to the arts is necessary or desirable, the question then arises in our minds whether such support will be given to institutions that serve only a highly select three or four percent of the population. Baumol and Bowen speak to this point:

> The outlook for government support depends to a considerable extent on the ability of the advocates of such support

[2] *Marvin Clawson, quoted in* ibid., *p. 78.*
[3] *William J. Baumol and William G. Bowen,* Performing Arts: The Economic Dilemma. *New York, The Twentieth Century Fund, 1966.*

to make an effective case for their position. But no matter what arguments are advanced, the amount of support provided will not be settled on the basis of abstract principles alone. The political realities are sure to play an important role. One of the apparent disadvantages of the arts in this respect is the fact that they currently attract interest and support only from a small minority of the population.[4]

Ignoring the ethical and legal questions involved, the political realities would seem to indicate that the arts must make their audiences more truly reflect society if they are going to make an effective case for increased government support. Many congressmen and other government officials will have difficulty, by their standards, in justifying major appropriations for the arts unless it can be proved that substantial progress is being made toward serving the many rather than the few.

There is a third reason why we believe it is desirable to broaden the base of the audience for theatre, and for the performing arts generally. This has to do with the effect of audience upon the art itself. There has been much comment about the lack of vitality in contemporary American theatre—particularly in the development of playwrights and a dynamic literature for theatre. The theatrical experience is the joint creation of playwright, company, and audience. It is difficult for us to see how American theatre can be a dynamic reflection of its society if its audience is not. Perhaps in the past, when only a small minority of the population had the means or education to be a part of theatre audience, or had any real influence on the total culture of their times, a dynamic theatre was able to grow from a limited audience base. But if this nation's culture is to be influenced by a majority of the population, then it seems that audiences must reflect this majority if we expect a vital theatre to emerge.

If there is necessity, as we believe, to seek ways to make audiences reflective of a cross-section of society, the question becomes: Is it possible, and if so, how? We are convinced that it *is* possible to penetrate the Cultural Curtain and to broaden as well as to enlarge the audience. We are further convinced

[4] Ibid.

that it can be done *without* compromising artistic standards of quality or altering the nature of the work. It is possible that the art may eventually be altered by the changing nature of the audience, but a change in the art need not precede a change in its public.

To broaden the base of the audience will take time, money, and innovation in people, ideas, and action—and, indeed, in the institutions themselves. Too many artistic institutions of this country seem to exhibit a "public be damned" attitude that is conducive neither to enlarging nor to broadening audiences. The impression is given that the proprietors are the sole discoverers of wisdom, beauty, and truth. The public, which is expected to come and worship at the shrine, is merely tolerated.

This impression must be reversed. The arts must adapt modern methods to make purchasing tickets and attending performances as easy and convenient as other aspects of modern life are becoming. The arts must spend the money and effort and apply good manners to make the public feel as welcome and comfortable as an individual would make a respected friend feel in his home.

The existing image of the arts is a formidable obstacle to enlarging and broadening audience. It is far too high-society, long-haired intellectual, artsy and sissy in our opinion. If this public image of the arts is inaccurate and differs from reality, then work has to be done to get the image in focus with reality. This can be done through enlightened understanding of the problem by arts management and with concerted public relations efforts by individual institutions. But such a monumental job must also be complemented by a major public relations effort on behalf of the arts on a *national* level. If, however, the present public image of the arts is already in focus with reality, or nearly so, then the arts institutions themselves must be changed with gradual—but drastic—innovations in this public policy and management which will not affect artistic standards or policy.

In order to broaden and enlarge audiences, artistic institutions must penetrate the Cultural Curtain. They must find ways to communicate with the majority of the population who will not listen because they have been intimidated into believing the arts are not for them. This cannot be done with traditional techniques of promotion and press agentry, nor by personnel who are rooted in these traditions. It can only be done with new ideas, new thinking, and new people. If the Noes will not come to our theatres, concert halls, and museums, then we must go to the Noes with all of our resources and talent. We must personally contact them through ever-widening circles of dedicated evangelists involving more and more members of our communities. If the Noes will not come to us because they have a fear of strangeness, then we must make the strange become familiar to them; we must take artistic experiences to them in places which are familiar to them and in terms which are meaningful to them. We must create new kinds of touring units and imaginative audiovisual presentations. We must, for example, create programs of Bible readings for churches, appropriate presentations for union halls, and programs of readings, scenes, and songs for the 4-H, Kiwanis, PTA's and Lions Clubs. All of this calls for drastic change in the nature of artistic institutions. In our opinion, the time has passed when a theatre can say that the *only* important thing is what happens on stage. At this time and in this country it seems that what must be taken to the people to "open the doors at least a crack" is just as important. The highest quality production is a failure without a vital audience—and an audience which is not representative of a vital society is not a vital one.

Stated most simply, we cannot expect to have attention paid to us by every part of the community unless we first pay attention to every part of the community. The key is a desire to *serve* instead of a compulsion to be worshipped. And it is this desire to serve which eventually creates within the total community an environment conducive to the total development, expression, and public support of the artistic institution. The task is a difficult one. It cannot be accomplished without some radical changes in philosophy on the part of most arts institutions. It will take boards of directors who see their community as well as their business responsibilities. It will take management and staff who are better trained, better paid, and experienced far beyond the narrow world of culture. It will take management and a board who understand that public relations is not press agentry but community service. Board and management must come to realize that the public and the institution's relations with it must be considered in every major policy decision.

Broadening the base of audience for the arts will also need a concerted national effort in research, public relations, and education. There is a desperate need for more knowledge about audience characteristics, including the attitudes and the psychological barriers to the arts. No single institution has the time or money to investigate these characteristics. There is an even greater need for an extensive program of public education through mass media and person-to-person contact to show people how the arts can be rewarding in their lives. It seems imperative that arts institutions find funds and a structure for meeting these needs.

But eventually, the challenge of audience development must be met on the level of imaginative new concepts created by the public relations and community-service staffs of the individual arts institutions themselves. We must find more people in the field, better trained, and more experienced in the ways of marketing, research, promotion, and communication. We must be ready to pay more to get them, and then we must let them have a free hand to use their imagination and experience, to introduce new concepts and to carry them through.

Finally, the challenge can only be met when everyone connected with the arts realizes that they must all be part of the ever-widening circles of dedicated evangelists personally communicating their enthusiasm for something in which they believe. Thus, only by "opening the doors at least a crack" for the majority of this country's people can the arts hope to be successful in their search for audience.

Appendix

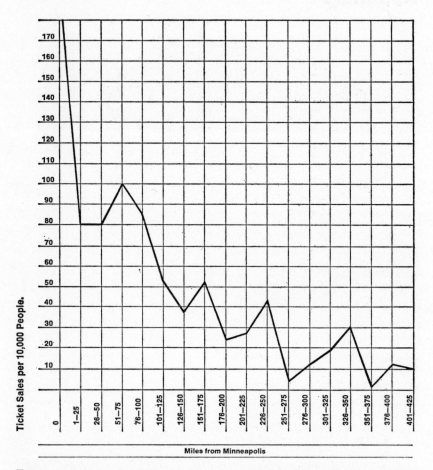

Figure 1. Opera ticket sales per 10,000 population. Using these statistics for the Midwest, The Minnesota Theatre Company was able to estimate its audience potential according to its geographical distribution.

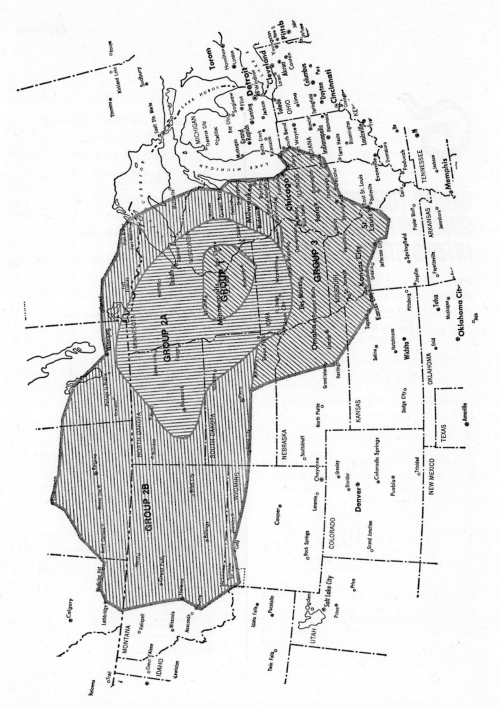

Figure 2. Geographical distribution of the Tyrone Guthrie Theatre's estimated audience potential.

WOULD YOU GIVE US SOME IMPORTANT INFORMATION & ADVICE?

Please fill out at intermission and deposit in boxes provided in lobbies or hand to an usher.

If this unique venture in professional repertory is successful, it may well lead the way to a bright new era in theatre for the whole United States. But to be successful it must attract, please and entertain you and thousands of others in the Midwest. We're trying to determine how we're doing.

Every tenth person in today's audience has received this questionnaire. It will be extremely valuable to us if you would take two minutes at intermission to fill it out and deposit it in one of the boxes provided in the lobbies.

Just check the appropriate spaces below. We would also appreciate any additional comments you care to make at the end. No need to sign your name unless you want to.

Thank you.

Oliver Rea

Oliver Rea
Administrative Director

NOTE: *Even if someone in your party has filled out this questionnaire at a previous performance, we would appreciate your filling it out now. If, through some coincidence, you personally received one at another performance, please give this to another member of your current party.*

1. Where is your current home? *(Check one)*

Minneapolis and Suburbs _____

St. Paul and Suburbs _____

Outside Twin Cities area
but within 100 miles _____

Elsewhere in Minnesota *(over 100 miles from Twin Cities)*, South Dakota, North Dakota, Montana, or Manitoba _____

Wisconsin, Illinois, Iowa, Kansas, Nebraska or Missouri _____

Elsewhere in the U.S.A. or Canada _____

ALSO: Please fill in

CITY _____ ZONE ____ STATE _____

2. What is the price of your seat and how was it purchased?

a. PRICE: *(Check one)*

$1.50 _____ $4.00 _____

$2.50 _____ $5.00 _____

b. TYPE: *(Check one)*

Season Ticket _____

Single Performance _____

c. HOW PURCHASED: *(Check one)*

Mail order from Guthrie Theatre _____

Mail order from Dayton's _____

Mail order from Field Schlick _____

In Person at Guthrie Theatre _____

In Person at Dayton's _____

Through a theatre party group _____

Other (specify): _____

3. What is your approximate age? *(Check one)*

Under 18 _____

18-25 _____

26-35 _____

36-49 _____

50 or over _____

4. And are you ...

a. Male_____ or Female_____

b. Married_____ or Unmarried_____

c. If married, are you with your husband or wife
Yes_____   No_____

5. Which one of these classifications best describe your present occupation, business or profession?

Student _____

Housewife _____

Retired _____

Professional *(Dr., Lawyer, Musician, Teacher, etc.)* _____

Business (Executive, owner, sales, etc.)_____

Sales Clerk/Clerical/Secretarial _____

Craftsman/Foreman/Worker _____

Technical/Engineering _____

Farmer _____

Not Employed _____

Other (specify):_____

6. What is the last grade in school you completed? *(Check one even if you're still in school.)*

8 or less _____

9-11 _____

12 *(high school graduate)* _____

Attended college, did not graduate _____

Four year college graduate _____

Post graduate _____

Other (specify):_____

7. Last year (1962) ...

a. Did you attend any plays, other than high school class plays, but including musical comedies, local theatre groups, etc.?
Yes_____   No_____

b. If yes: Approximately how many?_____

c. About how many of these were in Minneapolis or St. Paul?_____

(OVER)

8. Last year *(1962)* did you attend any of the following kinds of attractions? *(Check those attended)*

Symphony concerts _____ Jazz concerts _____

Pro baseball games _____ Pro football games _____

Operas _____   Ballets _____

9a. How are you enjoying today's performance?

Extremely well _____, very well _____,
fairly well _____, not too well _____, or
not at all _____.

b. How does this compare with what you expected?

Better _____, about the same _____, or
not as well _____.

10. When the season is over, how many of the four plays do you expect you will have seen?

One_____; Two_____; Three_____; Four_____.

11. If you would like, please give us any specific comments you have about the Tyrone Guthrie Theatre and the play you are seeing today.

_____

_____

_____

_____

_____

_____

_____

_____

_____

Figure 3. Questionnaire used in the 1963 audience-analysis survey. Study findings are reported in Table 1 which follows.

TABLE 1.

An Analysis
Of Those Attending the Guthrie Theatre
During 1962–1963[a]

Question 1: Where is your current home?
(Base: 10,408)

Minneapolis and suburbs	52.5%
St. Paul and suburbs	15.4
Outside Twin Cities area but within 100 miles	9.4
Elsewhere in Minnesota, S. Dakota, N. Dakota, Montana, or Manitoba	6.6
Wisconsin, Illinois, Iowa, Kansas, Nebraska, or Missouri	7.7
Elsewhere in the U.S.A. or Canada	7.9
Outside the U.S.A. or Canada	.3

Question 2a: What is the price of your seat?
(Base: 10,241)

$1.50	10.2%
2.50	26.5
4.00	35.7
5.00	27.5
Other prices	.1

Question 2b: Type of ticket bought
(Base: 10,157)

Season ticket	42.6%
Single performance ticket	57.4

Question 2c: How was it (the ticket) purchased?
(Base: 10,232)

Mail order from Guthrie Theatre	30.8%
Mail order from Dayton's	21.6
Mail order from Field-Schlick	1.3
In person at Guthrie Theatre	22.1
In person at Dayton's	11.3
Through a theatre-party group	5.0
Other (e.g., gifts, phone, etc.)	7.9

Question 3: What is your approximate age?
(Base: 10,382)

under 18	5.7%
18–25	17.8
26–35	25.7
36–49	27.3
50 or over	23.4

Question 4a: And are you male or female?
(Base: 10,020)

Female	55.4%
Male	44.6

Question 4b: And are you married or unmarried?
(Base: 9,644)

Married	64.3%
Unmarried (e.g. Single persons, divorced, widowed)	35.7

Question 4c: If married, are you with your husband or wife?
(Base: 6,011) b

Yes	80.3%
No	19.7

*Question 5: Which one of these classifications best describes
your present occupation, business or profession?*
(Base: 10,398)

Professional	31.2%
Housewife	22.9
Student	17.9
Business	12.8
Sales clerk/clerical/secretarial	4.7
Technical/engineering	3.7
Retired	3.6
All others	2.7
Unemployed	.4

Question 6: What is the last grade in school you completed?
(Base: 10,358)

Grammar school or less	1.3%
Some high school	4.7
High-school graduate	11.6

Some college	19.2%
College graduate	28.9
Post graduate	32.7
Other (e.g., business school, nursing, etc.)	3.3

Question 7: Last year (1962), did you attend any plays, other than high school class plays, but including musical comedies, local theatre groups, etc?
(Base: 10,322)

Yes, one or more plays was attended	82.9%
No plays, etc. were attended in 1962	17.1

Question 7b: (If plays, etc. were attended in 1962, ask:)
Approximately how many did you attend?
(Base: 8,185) c

1	9.5%
2–4	43.9
5–8	27.9
9 or more	18.2
Don't remember	.5

Question 7c: (If plays, etc. were attended in 1962, ask:)
About how many of these were in Minneapolis or St. Paul?
(Base: 7,910)

All were seen in Twin Cities	49.2%
More than half were seen in Twin Cities	10.4
Half	4.0
Less than half	7.4
None	28.8
Don't remember	.2

Question 8: Last year (1962) did you attend any of the following kinds of attractions . . . symphony concerts, pro baseball games, operas, pro football games, ballets, or jazz concerts? Which?
(Base: 8,898) d

Symphony concerts	65.8%
Pro baseball games	55.8
Operas	33.7
Pro football games	28.3
Ballets	24.0
Jazz concerts	19.2

Question 9a: How are you enjoying today's performance—
extremely well, very well, fairly well, not too well, or not at
all?
(Base: 9,333)

Extremely well satisfied	53.6%
Very well satisfied	34.2
Fairly well satisfied	9.5
Not too well satisfied	2.1
Not at all satisfied	.6

Question 9b: How does this compare with what you expected:
Better, about the same, or not as well?
(Base: 8,948)

Better	51.0%
About the same	43.3
Not as well	5.6

Question 10: When the season is over, how many of the four
plays do you expect you will have seen?
(Base: 9,854)

1	18.5%
2	19.3
3	12.6
4	49.5
Don't know	.2

Source: Compiled by Twin Cities Marketing and Research Department
Batten, Barton, Durstine and Osborn, Inc., 1963–1964.

Notes:
  [a] Total sample: 10,421. Bases given for each question represent the
respondents who answered the question.
  [b] All married people who answered this question.
  [c] Excludes 1,764 respondents not eligible to answer this question, as
well as 472 eligibles who failed to respond.
  [d] Percents exceed 100 due to multiple answers.

TABLE 2

Comparison of *Minnesota Theatre Company Audience* (1963) With the Profile of U.S. Performing Arts Audience[a]

		U.S. Performing Arts Audience		Minnesota Theatre Company (1963)
Sex				
	Male	52.8%		44.6%
	Female	47.2		55.4
Age				
	Under 20	6.9	Under 18	5.7
	20–60	81.4	18–50	70.9
	Over 60	9.0	Over 50	23.4
Occupational Category				
	Males employed	86.1		77.4
	Professionals	63.0		51.0
	Managerial	21.4		30.5
	Blue Collar	2.6		6.3
	(Other categories not comparable)			
	Male students	13.9		20.4
			Retired	2.2
	Females employed	49.7		41.0
	Professionals	63.2		57.3
	Managerial	7.2		8.0
	Clerical	24.9		10.0
	Blue Collar	1.9		4.6
	(Other categories not comparable)			
	Female students	15.1		16.9
	Housewives	35.2		42.1

Education

Males (age 25 and over)		(All Respondents)
Grade school and less than 4 years high school	2.8%	5.8%
4 years high school	15.3	7.6
1–3 years college	23.6	15.2
4 years college	23.1	25.4
Graduate school	31.6	45.0
Females (age 25 and over)		(All Respondents)
Grade school and less than 4 years high school	2.8	6.7
4 years high school	15.3	15.0
1–3 years college	23.6	22.9
4 years college	26.7	30.1
Graduate school	31.6	32.0

Frequency of Attendance

Average number of theatre performances attended in last 12 months	8.4	5.2

Sources: Minnesota Theatre Company statistics compiled by Twin Cities Marketing and Research Department of Batten, Barton, Durstine and Osborn, Inc., 1963–1964. U.S. Performing Arts Audience reported in William J. Baumol and William G. Bowen, *Performing Arts: The Economic Dilemma,* New York, Twentieth Century Fund, 1966.

Note: a "U.S. Performing Arts Audience" *refers to composite characteristics of American audiences in 1965, as compiled from the nation-wide survey conducted under the auspices of the Twentieth Century Fund.*

TABLE 3.

The Four Seasons' Statistics of the Minnesota Theatre
Company

Plays Performed	Number of Performances	Attendance	Percent Capacity
1963			
Hamlet (Shakespeare)	46	50,006	75.6
The Miser (Molière)	42	52,335	82.5
The Three Sisters (Chekhov)	31	39,804	89.3
Death of a Salesman (Miller)	33	41,786	88.5
Total:	152	183,931	84.2
1964			
Henry V (Shakespeare)	46	51,111	77.3
Saint Joan (Shaw)	47	58,138	86.0
The Glass Menagerie (Williams)	42	49,315	81.7
Volpone (Jonson)	46	56,066	84.8
Total:	181	214,630	82.5
1965			
Richard III (Shakespeare)	52	56,358	75.4
The Way of the World (Congreve)	44	40,649	64.3
The Cherry Orchard (Chekhov)	54	59,340	76.5
The Caucasian Chalk Circle (Brecht)	38	48,375	88.6
The Miser (Molière)	26	35,111	94.0
Total:	214	239,833	78.0
1966			
As You Like It (Shakespeare)	51	54,689	74.6
The Skin of Our Teeth (Wilder)	50	56,412	78.5

The Dance of Death			
(Strindberg)	30	32,148	74.6
S. S. Glencairn (O'Neill)	45	30,481	47.1
The Doctor's Dilemma			
(Shaw)	47	40,442	59.9
Total:	223	214,172	66.8

Bibliography

Baird, Russel N. and Turnbull, Arthur T., *Industrial and Business Journalism*, Philadelphia, Chilton Company, 1961.

Baumol, William J. and Bowen, William G., *Performing Arts: The Economic Dilemma*, New York, Twentieth Century Fund, 1966.

Cutlip, Scott M. and Center, Allen H., *Effective Public Relations*, Englewood Cliffs, N.J., Prentice-Hall, 1964.

Ferguson, Rowena, *Editing the Small Magazine*, New York, Columbia University Press, 1958.

Guthrie, Sir Tyrone, *A New Theatre*, New York, McGraw-Hill, 1964.

Lesly, Philip (ed.), *Public Relations Handbook*, Englewood Cliffs, N.J., Prentice-Hall, 1962.

Pratt, K. C., *House Magazine Layout*, Hamilton, Ohio, Champion Paper and Fibre Company, 1947.

Price, Matlack, *Advertising and Editorial Layout*, New York, McGraw-Hill, 1949.

Rockefeller Panel Report, *The Performing Arts: Problems and Prospects*, New York, McGraw-Hill, 1965.

Root, Robert, *Modern Magazine Editing*, Dubuque, Iowa, Wm. C. Brown Company, 1966.

Wales, Hugh G., Gentry, Dwight L., and Wales, Max., *Advertising Copy, Layout and Typography*, New York, Ronald Press, 1958.

WESTMAR COLLEGE LIBRARY.